CRACOW LANDSCAPE MONOGRAPHS

1

INSTITUTE OF ARCHAEOLOGY
JAGIELLONIAN UNIVERSITY IN KRAKÓW

INSTITUTE OF LANDSCAPE ARCHITECTURE
CRACOW UNIVERSITY OF TECHNOLOGY

CRACOW LANDSCAPE MONOGRAPHS 1

**Landscape as impulsion for culture:
research, perception & protection**

DEFINITIONS, THEORY & CONTEMPORARY
PERCEPTION OF LANDSCAPE

Kraków 2016

CRACOW LANDSCAPE MONOGRAPHS
VOL. 1

REVIEWER
Beata Kwiatkowska-Kopka

VOLUME EDITOR
Piotr Kołodziejczyk

COVER DESIGN
Katarzyna Kołodziejczyk

PROOFREADING
Piotr Kołodziejczyk
Izabela Sykta

TEXT DESIGN
Elżbieta Fidler-Źrałka

ISSN 2451-1692
ISBN 978-83-942469-4-5

Publishers:

Institute of Archeology
Jagiellonian University in Kraków
Gołębia 11 str., 31-007 Kraków, Poland
www.clc.edu.pl

Institute of Landscape Architecture
Cracow University of Technology
Warszawska 24 str., 31-155 Kraków, Poland
www.architektura-krajobrazu.pk.edu.pl

CONTENTS

INTRODUCTION

Piotr Kołodziejczyk[1], Beata Kwiatkowska-Kopka[2]
[1]Jagiellonian University in Kraków, Institute of Archaeology;
[2]Departament of Archaeological Reserve and Lapidarium, Wawel Royal Castle State Collection of Art

The landscape is a living, delicate fabric, imbued with the memories and energy of the past and present generations. It is a space of our individual and social functioning, a basic system for all human activities. Natural processes intertwine with the effects of human activity in a landscape, forming together what is known as the cultural landscape. Typically, a cultural landscape is understood as being comprised of parts of an animate and an inanimate nature and those of human works which are fixed permanently in the landscape. This definition may be enriched by adding that another important element of a cultural landscape are the relations between its particular components. This is important, as a cultural landscape was previously far too often perceived as just an aggregate of monuments, a great oversimplification. The broader understanding of cultural landscape should embrace elements of an animate and inanimate nature, the relics of human activity relatively permanently connected with the landscape, the relations between these component, as well as the meanings given to them. Understood in this way, a cultural landscape is a kind of a synthesis of the cultural heritage of man, their attitude to nature and to those monuments that have survived in the landscape and influence our perception and understanding of the surrounding world.

With the advent of human culture the unintentional and intentional shaping of the landscape also began. The millennia of development and changes generated new factors affecting spatial transformations and their formation and influence on our environment continues to this day, often being a phenomenon deeply rooted in the past of particular places or human groups. A cultural landscape builds identity and its memory matrix. Collective memory and collective identity have many dimensions and operate on many levels. They may be an attribute of a group, but also of an individual. And being the attribute of an individual, they may refer to, or be constructed by, many communities of various kinds at the same time (national, regional, local, family, associational). Each of them can provide the individual with different ranges of memory as well. Memory and space are profoundly contextual – they depend on the culture and place in which they are rooted. Is it therefore possible to have one answer to the question of what the broadly understood landscape space is and what are its elements? This answer must be dependent on the cultural matrix of a given community, and the same should apply to our research and preservation activity.

Multidisciplinary landscape studies create a unique opportunity to trace environmental and cultural transformations and bring us closer to understanding the distance that mankind has covered over the thousands years of its existence on the surface of the Earth. This is because the cultural "multi-layer structure" is an inherent feature of landscape, making it a kind of palimpsest. The multidimensional perception of the landscape makes it possible to identify the many and various ways in which it impacts our life.

We invite you to participate in the first edition of the Cracow Landscape Conference and the accompanying series of monographs devoted to landscape-related issues, broadly understood. During our meetings we will attempt to bring together the efforts of specialists representing various disciplines that investigate, interpret and create landscapes. We will discuss definitions and the understanding of landscape-related issues among people from different cultural milieus as well as the role of landscape studies in examining the human past. Moreover, we will analyse the contemporary perception of landscape and methods of its protection and transformation because the landscape constitutes a permanent challenge and unending task for all of us.

The main objective of the CLC cycle meetings and the accompanying publishing series is the theoretical and practical analysis of landscapes and their particular elements in various parts of the world, as well as the identification and interpretation of contexts, connections, morphology, and arrangement of material relics and intangible phenomena that nevertheless left their imprint in landscape. Our goal is a more comprehensive understanding and explanation of human behaviours and historical processes, both in a distant past and in more recent times, which have left their unique imprint on the landscape.

The discussion we plan to initiate will be distinguished by a complementary research approach, bringing together methods from humanities, natural sciences, exact sciences, as well as art sciences and technical sciences. Such an approach offers an opportunity to integrate different research perspectives oriented on investigating the "man-environment" interaction, the role of man in landscape transformations, and of landscape in shaping the patterns and mechanisms of culture. There were many shades and motives to these mutual interactions and relations, which in many aspects influenced human existence and shaped the present day picture of culture and environment.

In our opinion, it is of particular importance to have among the participants of the meetings and publications those who create landscapes today. It is the responsibility of landscape architecture to create the space we live in and create beauty around us. This value, currently at risk, requires protection and development according to commonly accepted rules. The latter, in turn, should be formulated and actualised through the investigation of landscapes of all types and kinds. This goal can be achieved only by the integration of the contributions from all the specialists and researchers involved in the shaping, researching, description and perception of landscape-related issues.

In our discussion, we would also like to address difficult but important issues related to current research, tendencies, and threats. We are firmly convinced that the work of landscape architects must be rooted deeply in the knowledge of the landscape's past, and its components. It must be concerned with both research and protection, encompassing both the natural and the anthropogenic components of landscape. Furthermore, one must not forget the most volatile and at the same time most endangered elements of cultural landscape, which are the traces of the intangible heritage of the past. Their exceptional value, which has become increasingly appreciated in recent years, requires exceptional care, research, and protection.

We are also going to highlight worthwhile projects and actions undertaken in historical objects, in hitherto undeveloped landscape, as well as in existing architectural complexes. A particular place in these studies will be accorded to parks and gardens, and all green areas, which still have too few defenders while being recently under immense pressure from public and private development. In this context it is worth emphasising once again our interest in the holistic definition of 'environment', understood as the set of interrelated animate and inanimate elements, including natural ones as well as those created by man.

We believe there is an urgent need to integrate the actions undertaken for the benefit of the environment with those focused on cultural heritage, which today are often realised independently and, as such, often ineffective. Thus, within the scope of our interest we will also include the elements of ecology and ecological awareness, as well as attempts to define the limits of human intervention in nature, especially in protected areas.

We invite you to join the discussion, hoping to build a strong and creative platform for exchanging reflections and information beneficial for the progress in research and the protection of the most valuable elements of landscape.

ASSESSMENT OF LANDSCAPE AND LANDSCAPE IN ASSESSMENT. LANDSCAPE AS A DETERMINANT OF REAL ESTATE VALUE

Agnieszka Szczepańska

University of Warmia and Mazury in Olsztyn, Department of Planning and Spatial Engineering

ABSTRACT

Landscape is an environmental resource. Environmental elements undergo evaluation and assessment, and various assessment methods have been proposed by environmental economics. The hedonic pricing method is one of such techniques. This indirect methodis applied on the assumption that the demand for a market good (real estate) is correlated with the supply of an environmental good (landscape). Landscape is an example of an environmental resource which shapes real estate prices. Feedback exists between the two elements: constituent elements of real estate make up landscape, and landscape shapes the value of real estate. As a factor that influences property value, landscape should be taken into account during appraisals of real estates, in particular real estates with residential and recreational functions. This article discusses the principles for assessing the market value of real estate with residential functions in view of its landscape attributes. The analysis was conducted on the example of building plots in suburban Olsztyn which are characterized by high scenic value.

Keywords
environmental good, landscape, market value, real estate

1. INTRODUCTION

1.1. Landscape and landscape components

Landscape is a multi-dimensional system with a specific structure and internal connections (Balon 2009). In the contemporary approach, landscape is regarded as a reflection of natural phenomena that take place without human involvement as well as anthropogenic processes in the geographic environment. According to Degórski (2014:54-55), landscape is a complex spatial structure shaped by human activity which directly impacts the natural environmentand leads to the dynamic development of environmental components, and where an integrated network of natural, urban, industrial, infrastructural and cultural components creates a landscape mosaic that is unique to a given natural and social environment. The above definition points to the existence of mutual correlations and feedback between natural and anthropogenic components of landscape.

For the needs of the consumer market, landscape is defined in environmental terms. In landscape ecology and physical geography, landscape generally denotes the natural environment. The key components of landscape, defined as an external manifestation of the geographic environment, are: geological structure, surface features/relief, surface water, soil, flora, fauna, land cover, climate and land use (Rylke 2010: 222-223). This approach postulates the existence of specific landscape components, including elements of inanimate and animate nature. The discussed concept is subjective because it applies only to the outward appearance of landscape which is judged based on the subjective perceptions of individuals (Kistowski 2014). The largely subjective concept of scenic value does not contradict the natural value of landscape which is evaluated with the use of various methods because humans have evolved in natural surroundings and abide by the principles of "natural law", i.e. values that are derived from the nature of the world (Rylke 2010). The outward appearance of landscape is perceived subjectively by humans through the senses. In the environmental approach, individual perceptions of landscape influence demand and determine the subjective value of space that surrounds real estate located in a "specific scenery". In this approach, landscape is evaluated mainly based on environmental components. According to González and Leon (2003: 160-161), "landscapes would refer to those properties of the environment which can be visually perceived, and the value of a particular landscape would be given by the satisfaction experienced in its contemplation".

1.2. Landscape as an economic good. Value of landscape

Landscape is an environmental resource, and from the point of view of economic theory, the environment is a specific resource which has economic value for consumers. In line with the total economic value (TEV) concept, the value derived by consumers from natural resources can be classified as use value and non-use value (Zawilińska 2014). Use value can be further divided into direct and indirect use value, where indirect use value is obtained through a non-removable product in nature. Non-use value is assigned to economic goods which are not used and will not be used by the present generation. Non-use value may include bequest value and existence value. In a similar approach, environmental resources can be assigned the following types of value (Górko and Poskrobko, 1991; Żylicz 1989; Woś 1995):
- use value – value derived from a given resource by the person performing the appraisal,
- option value – willingness to pay for a resource to preserve an option of potential future use,
- altruistic value – willingness to pay for a resource which is used by other people,
- existence value – the benefit received from knowing that a given resource exists.

Those value categories make up the overall value of environmental resources (full economic value), where use value is a category that is easiest to evaluate and assess.

The methods of evaluating non-market commodities are based on artificial market structures and can be divided into two groups: hypothetical markets and surrogate markets. This classification is responsible for two approaches to environmental resource assessment (Żylicz 2007; Folmer, Gabel and Opschoor, 1996). Direct methods rely on hypothetical data obtained from consumer surveys. During such interviews, consumers indicate the price they would be willing to pay for different environmental components, and their responses are used to create a hypothetical market (which does not exist in reality). It is assumed that consumers can consciously describe their preferences, and the value of environmental resources is estimated based on the provided information. It should be noted that non-use values can be assessed only with hypothetical market methods which are applied when indirect methods cannot be used.

In the indirect approach, environmental resources are assessed in view of market commodities. This approach relies on the assumption that commodities do not exist on their own, but are influenced by goods on an organized market which shapes the price of those assets, including landscape and real estate. The consumption of environmental resources is related to the supply of market goods, and the prices quoted on the market reflect the value of environmental resources perceived by consumers. The value of a non-market commodity is determined based on information about changes in demand for a market good and changes in the availability of environmental assets. Landscape is a typical example of a non-market commodity. As an environmental resource, landscape has a certain value, but it cannot be purchased on the market (there are no demand and supply curves for landscape because a landscape market does not exist). Therefore, landscape can only be purchased in combination with a market good, namely real estate. Landscape is a non-market commodity, but it is an economic good because buyers are willing to pay for real estate characterized by high scenic value. Therefore, the value of landscape is "hidden" in the value of the accompanying market commodity, i.e. real estate. As a non-market commodity, landscape influences the well-being or quality of life in households that "consume" market commodities such as residential and recreational property. In indirect methods, the value of the environment is determined based on the prices of market goods and services such as land and apartments. Those prices can vary depending on the condition of the environment in which they are situated. The prices of real estate increase with the attractiveness of its surroundings (Korporowicz 2003).

The hedonic pricing method is an example of an indirect method. It is used to adjust price indices based on changes in product quality (Widłak 2010). The benefits derived from environmental services are expressed in monetary terms by evaluating the influence that those services have on the prices of the related goods and services. The hedonic pricing method is applied on the assumption that the price paid for a commodity is determined by the characteristic features of that commodity. The consumption of market goods is linked with the supply of environmental commodities. Therefore, the value of a non-market commodity can be determined based on changes in demand for a market commodity which are induced by changes in the availability (quality) of environmental resources (Zygmuntowicz 2006). Non-market attributes are assessed based on transacted goods in which the evaluated attribute is expressed with different intensity. According to Schaeffer (2008:146), "market prices are attractive measures of the value of resources because they are usually readily available and, if certain conditions are met, have desirable characteristics". The price of a market commodity can be expressed as a sum of its attributes, where environmental features are one of such attributes (Folmer, Gabel and Opschoor, 1996).

The price of landscape, a non-market environmental commodity, is hidden in the price of a market commodity, and it partially explains the variations in real estate prices. Buyers pay for landscape when purchasing real estate, and the price of landscape is hidden in the market price of acquiredproperty (Bajerowski *et al.*, 2007). The value of the attribute that corresponds to landscape quality indicates the additional amount of money that a buyer would be willing to pay for real estate characterized by high scenic value. The influence of landscape on real estate prices can be estimated by comparing the prices of property that differ only in their scenic value. Landscape is always linked with location, therefore, its value can be reflected in the value of real estate that "responds" to scenic value, in particular residential and recreational property. The hedonic pricing method is applied mainly in analyses of the real estate market and in evaluations of environmental resources in an urban setting, but it can also be used in suburban areas characterized byhigh levels of residential development (Cellmer *et al.*, 2012). Suburban areas experience growing pressure from metropolitan centers due to progressing urban sprawl, but environmental resources in suburban areas are still an important determinant of the price of residential property.

1.3. Environmental factors and real estate value

The value of real estate is influenced by physical, environmental, economic, legal, demographic, political and social factors (Kucharska-Stasiak 2008). According to the Temporary Interpretation Guidelines for Domestic Appraisal Principles, entitled "The influence of environmental factors on real estate appraisal", environmental factors have to be taken into account during real estate appraisal. Environmental factors include the proximity of parks and recreational areas, transformed and non-transformed green spaces, and water bodies. Those features determine the quality of space surrounding real estate and significantly influence its value. The quality of living space is a major determinant of the quality of life, and humans instinctively choose residential locations characterized by high-quality space. The proximity of water bodies, green spaces and diversified relief are the key components of valuable landscape which contribute to a potential buyer's "first impression". Many people prefer esthetically pleasing environments, and esthetic information can have considerable economic impact (de Groot *et al.*, 2002). For this reason, landscape significantly influences the value of real estate, in particular the valueof residential and recreational property which should provide users with access to high-quality space. Strong relationships between environmental features and property prices have been observed on real estate markets (Anderson and West, 2006; Asmawi and Abdullah 2015; Borkowska *et al.*, 2001; Czembrowski and Kronenberg, 2016; Cellmer *et al.*, 2012; Geoghegan 2002; Irwin, 2002; Jim and Hen, 2005, 2007; Noor, Anderson and Cordell, 1988; Schläpfer *et al.* 2015; Tagliafierro *et al.* 2013).

2. INFLUENCE OF LANDSCAPE COMPONENTS ON THE VALUE OF RESIDENTIAL REAL ESTATE

2.1. Subject matter and spatial scope of the study

The relationship between the ecological value and the economic value of non-market commodities can be inversely proportional (the value of one variable increases when the value of the other variable decreases) or directly proportional (the value of one variable increases with an increase in the value of the other variable) (Zygmuntowicz, 2006). The presence of water bodies undoubtedly increases the scenic value of a residential area (Wen, Bu and Qin, 2014; Loures *et al.*, 2015). When the remaining parameters of a residential area are identical (general location, neighborhood, purpose, access to public transport, topographic features, etc.), the variations in the prices of real estate are determined by landscape attractiveness which is evaluated subjectively by prospective buyers.

In this study, the prices of building plots zoned for the construction of single-family homes were analyzed based on the presence of water bodies in the surrounding space. The plots are situated in the municipality of Stawiguda, a suburban area of the city of Olsztyn. The analyzed municipality has been undergoing rapid residential development, in particular single-family housing. The local real estate market is well developed, and it features a high number of transactions. The evaluated area is an attractive location due to the proximity of Olsztyn (capital city of the Region of Warmia and Mazury) and high-quality environmental factors, mostly lakes and forests which contribute to the attractiveness of the local landscape (Fig. 1). The analysis covered a residential estate situated around 10 km from downtown Olsztyn (Fig. 2).

In line with the land use plan of Stawiguda municipality for 2013, the analyzed area constitutes a Central Zone (S2) for residential construction (Fig. 3 and Fig. 4). The examined estate is situated in the direct vicinity of Lake Wulpińskie (area of 706.7 ha, water quality class I). Moraine hills and numerous islets contribute to the picturesque character of the local landscape. The lake is situated in a protected landscape area.

2.2. Methods and Results

The analysis was carried out on the assumption that due to the similarity of the remaining parameters, including location in the same residential estate, access to public transport, neighborhood and function, the scenic value of the examined area is determined by the proximity of the lake. The distance separating building plots from the lake was adopted as a variable in statistic analyses.

The analysis was performed in the following stages:
1. acquisition of source data (transaction prices, location of building plots),
2. determination of straight line distance between building plots and the lake,
3. development of a scatter plot of unit prices of building plots relative to their distance from the lake,
4. determination of linear correlations (correlation coefficient) between the prices of individual building plots and their distance from the lake,
5. spatial interpolation of individual transaction prices,

Detailed information about the location of the analyzed building plots was obtained from a topographic map and a master map available on the website of the Olsztyn County Office. Data were also acquired during a local survey. Information about market transactions involving land plots zoned for residential

Fig.1. Photographs of the analyzed area.
Source: Website of Stawiguda municipality, http://www.stawiguda.pl/gmina-z-lotu-ptaka

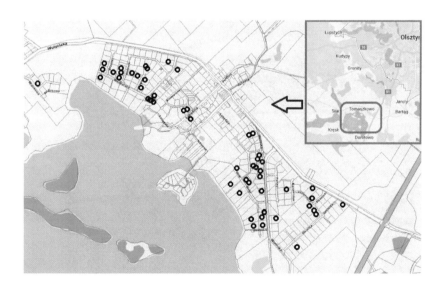

Fig.2. Location of the analyzed estate.
Source: Own elaboration based on the real estate cadaster of Olsztyn county http://powiatolsztynski.geoportal2.pl/

construction was obtained from the Register of Real Estate Prices and Values kept by the Center for Geodetic and Cartographic Resources of Olsztyn County. A total of 48 transactions conducted between 2009 and 2015 were analyzed. In the examined period, the prices of land ranged from PLN 80/m^2 to PLN 320/m^2 (mean price: PLN 138/m^2, standard deviation: PLN 45/m^2). The price rate of change indicator was determined at -0.2% per month, and prices were time-adjusted before calculations and interpolation.

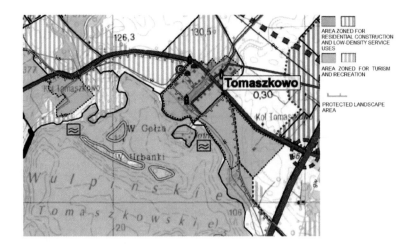

Fig.3. Land use types in the analyzed area.
Source: Land use plan of Stawiguda municipality.

Fig.4. Land use in the local zoning plan.
After: Geographic information system of Stawiguda municipality, http://sip.stawiguda.pl/mapa/

The scatter plots of unit prices of building plots relative to their distance from the lake are shown in Figure 4. The price of the analyzed plots clearly decreased with an increase in distance from the lake: the price decreased by PLN 0.17/ m^2 per every meter increasing the distance between the plot and the lake.

A linear correlation analysis revealed the presence of statistically significant correlations between the dependent variable (unit price) and the independent variable (distance from the lake) at -0.49. The observed relationship was inversely proportional – land prices decreased with an increase in distance from the lake (Table 1).

Table1. Linear correlations between the unit prices of building plots and the distance from the lake.
Prepared by author.

Variable	Linear correlations (unit prices of building plots– distance from lake) Correlation coefficients are significant at p < 0.05000; N=48			
	Mean	SD	Unit price [PLN/m²]	Distance from lake [m]
Unit price [PLN/m²]	137.46	44.85	1.00	-0.49
Distance from lake [m]	210.69	128.05	-0.49	1.00

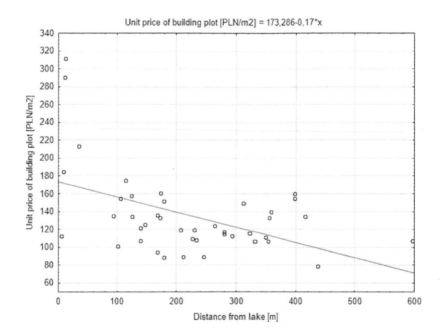

Fig.5. Distribution of unit prices of building plots relative to the distance from the lake.
Prepared by author.

The presence of inversely proportional relationships was confirmed by the interpolation of unit prices (Fig. 5). In general, the prices of land decreased with an increase in distance separating the plot from the lake. Local price hikes can be attributed to the fact that building plots situated in the examined estate are rarely put up for sale due to their attractiveness, and limited supply increases the prices of transacted property.

3. CONCLUSIONS

The study revealed that landscape components such as lakes significantly influence the prices of real estate. The presence of water bodies in the vicinity of real estate considerably affects the prices of building plots. Our findings confirm that prospective buyers pay attention to the attractiveness of the landscape

surrounding residential property. The prices of building plots situated in the immediate vicinity of a lake were significantly higher than the prices of plots situated further away from the water body. The results of this study indicate that landscape is an important determinant of the prices of property traded on the market.

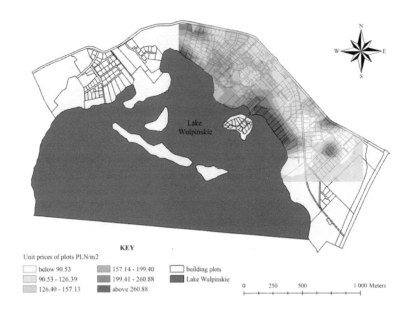

KEY

Unit prices of plots PLN/m2

below 90.53	157.14 - 199.40	building plots
90.53 - 126.39	199.41 - 260.88	Lake Wulpinskie
126.40 - 157.13	above 260.88	

0   250   500   1 000 Meters

Fig.6. Distribution of unit prices of building plots in the analyzed estate.
Prepared by author.

BIBLIOGRAPHY

Anderson, L., and Cordell, H. (1988). Influence of trees on residential property values in Athens, Georgia (USA): a survey based on actual sales prices. *Landscape and Urban Planning*, 15(1), pp.153-164.

Anderson, S. and West, S. (2006). Open space, residential property values, and spatial context. *Regional Science and Urban Economics*, 36(6), pp. 773-789

Bajerowski, T., Biłozor, A., Cieślak, I., Senetra, A. and Szczepańska, A. (2007). *Ocena i wycena krajobrazu.* Olsztyn: Educaterra.

Balon, J. (2009). Porządki przestrzenne – syntetyczna wizja krajobrazu. *Problemy Ekologii Krajobrazu.* XXIII, pp.61–70.

Borkowska, M., Rozwadowska, M., Śleszyński, J. and Żylicz, T. (2001). Environmental amenities on the housing market in Warsaw: hedonic price method research. Ekonomia, (3), pp. 70-82.

Cellmer, R., Senetra, A. and Szczepańska, A. (2012), Land Value Maps of Naturally Valuable Areas. *Geomatics and Environmental Engineering*, 6(3), pp.15-24. Czembrowski, P. and Kronenberg, J. (2016). Hedonic pricing and different urban green space types and sizes: Insights into the discussion on valuing ecosystem services. *Landscape and Urban Planning*, 146, pp. 11-19.

De Groot, R., Wilson M. and Boumans R. (2002). A typology for the classification, description and valuation

of ecosystem functions, goods and services. *Ecological Economics*, 41(3), pp. 393-408.

Degórski, M. (2014). Krajobraz jako odbicie przyrodniczych i antropogenicznych procesów zachodzących w megasystemie środowiska geograficznego. Problemy Ekologii Krajobrazu. 23(23), 53-60

Folmer, H., Gabel, L. and Opschoor, H. (1996). *Ekonomia środowiska i zasobów naturalnych*. Warszawa: Wydawnictwo Krupski i S-ka.

Fuerst, F. and McAllister, P. (2011). Green noise or green value? Measuring the effects of environmental certification on office values. *Real Estate Economics*, 39(1), pp.45-69.

Geoghegan, J. (2002). The value of open spaces in residential land use. Land use policy, 19(1), pp.91-98.

González, M., Leon, C.J., 2003. Consumption process and multiple valuation of landscape attributes. *Ecological Economics*, 45(2), pp. 159-169.

Górka, K. and Poskrobko, B. (1991). *Ekonomika ochrony środowiska*. Warszawa: PWE.

Irwin, E. G. (2002). The effects of open space on residential property values. *Land Economics*, 78(4), 465-480.

Jim C. and Chen, W. (2006). Impacts of urban environmental elements on residential housing prices in Guangzhou (China). *Landscape and Urban Planning*, 78(4), pp. 422-434.

Jim C. and Chen W. (2007). Consumption preferences and environmental externalities: A hedonic analysis of the housing market in Guangzhou. *Geoforum*, 38(2), pp. 414-431.

Kistowski, M. (2014). Koncepcja równowagi krajobrazu–mity i rzeczywistość. *Problemy Ekologii Krajobrazu*. 21(21), pp. 81-91

Korporowicz, V. (2003). Ekonomia środowiska - współczesna nauka z tradycjami. *Studia Ecologiae et Bioethicae*, 1/2003, pp. 329-340

Kucharska-Stasiak, E. (2008). *Nieruchomość w gospodarce rynkowej*. Warszawa: Wydawnictwo Naukowe PWN.

Loures, L., Loures, A., Nunes, J. and Panagopoulos, T. (2015). Landscape Valuation of Environmental Amenities throughout the Application of Direct and Indirect Methods. *Sustainability*, 7(1), pp.794-810.

Noor, N., Asmawi, M. and Abdullah, A. (2015). Sustainable Urban Regeneration: GIS and Hedonic Pricing Method in determining the value of green space in housing area. *Procedia-Social and BehavioralSciences*, 170, pp. 669-679.

Rylke, J. (2010). Rozpoznawanie i ocena wartości przyrodniczych i kulturowych na podstawie krajobrazu. In: J.Szyszko, J. Rylke, P. Jeżewski and I. Dymitryszyn, ed. *Ocena i wycena zasobów przyrodniczych*. Warszawa: Wydawnictwo SGGW, pp. 222-238.

Schaeffer, P.V. (2008). Thoughts concerning the economic valuation of landscapes. *Journal of Environmental Management*. 89(3), pp. 146-154.

Schläpfer, F., Waltert, F., Segura, L. and Kienast, F. (2015). Valuation of landscape amenities: A hedonic pricing analysis of housing rents in urban, suburban and periurban Switzerland. *Landscape and Urban Planning*, 141, pp. 24-40.

Standard VI.1 Wpływ czynników środowiskowych na wartość nieruchomości. Standardy Zawodowe Rzeczoznawców Majątkowych.(2004). Warszawa: Polska Federacja Stowarzyszeń Rzeczoznawców Majątkowych.

Studium uwarunkowań i kierunków zagospodarowania przestrzennego gminy Stawiguda.(2013) Załącznik nr 1 do Uchwały Nr XXVI/219/2013 Rady Gminy Stawiguda z dnia 27 czerwca 2013 r. [online] pages. Available at: http://www.stawiguda.pl/userfiles/Nieruchomosci/Studium_2013/2013_studium_stawigudatekst.pdf [Access 17 Jan. 2016]

Tagliafierro, C., Longo, A., Van Eetvelde, V., Antrop, M. and Hutchinson, W. (2013). Landscape economic valuation by integrating landscape ecology into landscape economics. *Environmental Science & Policy*, 32, pp. 26-36.

Wen, H., Bu, X. and Qin, Z. (2014). Spatial effect of lake landscape on housing price: A case study of the West Lake in Hangzhou, China. *Habitat International*, 44, pp. 31-40.

Widłak, M. (2010). Metody wyznaczania hedonicznych indeksów cen jako sposób kontroli zmian jakości dóbr. *Wiadomości Statystyczne*, (9), pp. 1-26.

Woś, A. (1995). *Ekonomika odnawialnych zasobów naturalnych*. Warszawa: Wydaw. Naukowe PWN.

Zawilińska, B. (2014). Ekonomiczna wartość obszarów chronionych. Zarys problematyki i metodyka badań. *Zeszyty Naukowe Uniwersytetu Ekonomicznego w Krakowie*, 12 (936), pp. 113-129.

Zygmuntowicz, Z. (2006). Tworzenie baz wiedzy dla wyceny dóbr nierynkowych w aspekcie określania wartosci rynkowej nieruchomosci. *Studia i Materiały Polskiego Stowarzyszenia Zarządzania Wiedzą*, 5, pp. 159-166.

Żylicz, T. (1989). Ekonomia wobec problemów środowiska przyrodniczego. Warszawa: Państwowe Wydawnictwo Naukowe PWN.Żylicz, T. (2007). Wycena dóbr nierynkowych. Aura (8), [online] pages. Available at: http://coin.wne.uw.edu.pl/tzylicz/0708AURA.pdf [Access 17 Jan. 2016], pp. 1-2.

PROGRESSIVE PRAGMATISM. THE NEXT GENERATION OF DUTCH LANDSCAPE DESIGN PRACTICES

Kees Lokman
University of British Columbia

ABSTRACT

As a small, densely populated country partially situated below sea level, the Dutch have a long history of manipulating the physical landscape. Current challenges in the Netherlands, including economic uncertainty, growing resource scarcity, energy transitions, and climate change, are providing new necessities and motivations for innovation in the realm of spatial design. This essay highlights emerging Dutch landscape design practices that answer this call and fundamentally engage these challenges. Projects discussed can be loosely divided into three categories: 1)strategic interventions marked by creative problem-solving and resourcefulness; 2)proposals focusing on urban metabolism by reconfiguring flows of water, waste, energy and materials; 3)projects that envision new climate change adaptation strategies. What characterizes all these projects is that they are at once pragmatic and progressive, generating solutions to actual and future challenges. The article concludes by describing how these projects can contribute to landscape design discourse globally.

Keywords
contemporary landscape architecture, strategic interventions, urban metabolism, climate change adaptation, spatial practices, the Netherlands

1. INTRODUCTION

Contemporary spatial practices in the Netherlands are still closely associated with the 'Super-Dutch'- a term coined by architecture critic Bart Lootsma to describe the innovative and provocative work generated by designers including Rem Koolhaas (OMA), Winy Maas (MVRDV) and Adriaan Geuze (West 8) in the 1990s and early 2000s (Lootsma 2000). Yet, while the Super-Dutch undeniably increased international visibility of Dutch design culture, their practices have also overshadowed a new generation of designers (Vanstiphout 2006). This generation has particularly taken off since the (European) economic recession and housing crisis of 2009. The crisis not only provided opportunities for Dutch designers to re-insert themselves into public debates but it also motivated a shift in modes of practice. Less concerned with iconography and wild eclecticism, this current generation of designers is particularly interested in social engagement, innovative funding models, strategic interventions and cross-scalar design approaches (Vanstiphout 2006). Designers are "becoming both developer and entrepreneur, creating their own commission situations, forming new cooperatives and providing ideas that are both inspiring and also practically applicable and feasible in difficult financial times" (van't Klooster 2013). And while recent publications, such as *Reactivate! Innovators of Dutch Architecture (2013)* have provided insights into the underlying practices and discourses shaping a new generation of Dutch architects, relatively little attention is given to recent landscape architecture projects in the Netherlands. As such, this article specifically looks at design methods and approaches developed by recent landscape design practices in the Netherlands. The projects discussed actively engage the topics of reuse, urban metabolism and climate change in attempts to generate productive multifunctional landscapes. The article concludes by describing how key design principles and approaches deployed in these projects can inform landscape design practices globally.

2. DUTCH PRAGMATISM

There are two distinct, yet interconnected, concepts that are important when discussing spatial design practices in the Netherlands. First, the *'polder model'* and second the idea of *'maakbaarheid'*. Both concepts are inherently connected to a fundamental belief in a democratic society, as well as humanity's ability to productively shape the built environment. Let us first look at the polder model concept.

2.1. The Polder Model

The need to manipulate the physical landscape is in the DNA of the Dutch (Salewski 2012). Exemplified by the saying: 'God created the earth, but the Dutch created the Netherlands', the Dutch have a long history of re-engineering and reconfiguring natural processes, particularly those related to water. Ever since the 9th century, the Dutch have constructed a complex network of dikes and numerous dams to manage and protect cities as well as to reclaim significant areas for agricultural use. During this period, the Dutch also developed different water management approaches in order to deal with flooding (van Tielhof 2015). Whereas flood protection was initially mainly a local matter, in the course of the early modern period-with the growing importance of cities and their hinterlands-it became increasingly critical to coordinate flood control among various stakeholders. Thus, different social classes and communities living in the same *polder*-a reclaimed area of land protected by a dike-had to come together to coordinate, fund and maintain the construction of appropriate flood control infrastructures. Over time, this notion of 'forced solidarity' led to the development of specialized regional institutions (water boards) to coordinate flood protection, preserve water quality and to manage the general water economy of their respective regions (de Mul and van den Berg 2011). Not surprisingly, the historic relationship with water has been a critical factor in shaping the Dutch *'polder model'*, which can be understood as a socio-political culture of consultation, consensus and compromise (de Vries 2014). While capitalism and immigration pressures have tested the limits of the polder model, the concept continues to influence spatial planning policy, which moves between decision-making processes on the national and local scale, with provinces (regional administrations) playing an intermediary role (Salewski 2012).

2.2. Maakbaarheid

In addition the polder model, another concept that has informed the form and functioning of the Dutch landscape is the notion of *maakbaarheid*. Directly translated, maakbaarheid means 'makeability', or "the ability to decide the form and future of one's physical environment" (Salewski 2012: 12). This utopian concept emerged in the 1960s and suggests the possibility to change social reality with the aid of certain instruments (Schuilenburg 2015). Vanstiphout and Provoost point out "these interventions consisted of equalising incomes and the education system in order to stimulate individuals from all classes to develop and educate themselves...Under the umbrella of the government, different parties, housing corporations, trade unions and entrepreneurs worked on creating an ideal model of society through planning" (Vanstiphout and Provoost 2009). At the time, rapid population growth, an emerging middle class and the discovery of the largest natural gas field of Europe in Groningen (1959) fuelled the belief in a *maakbare samenleving* (makeable society). Design disciplines were entrusted with envisioning new ways in which the built environment could contribute to important aspects of this makeable society. This included the development of new spatial concepts for two large reclaimed polders-Oost-Flevoland (1957) and Zuid-Flevoland (1968)-as well as the introduction of the living street (Woonerf, 1970s) as a new typology for urban design. However, by the mid-seventies, the idea that socially desirable behaviour could be shaped with aid of spatial design practices (social engineering) was increasingly met with criticism. And while the Dutch did abandon modernist planning principles, the notion that design has a role to play in shaping socio-cultural relations always remained (Salewski 2012). Recently, the 4th International Architectural Biennale in Rotterdam (IABR) reveals this on-going belief in a makeable society. In the curatorial statement, Kees Christiaanse argues: "Architecture's major challenge, in the eyes of the IABR, is to design and realize decent day-to-day living conditions for billions of people. With the theme Open City: Designing Coexistence, the 4th edition of the IABR places special emphasis on the social aspect of this challenge: how can architects and urban planners make concrete contributions to diversity, vitality, and liveability—in short, to the sustainability of the urban condition" (IABR 2009: 7). Contemporary Dutch design practices continue to explore this call for creating dynamic and just socio-spatial configurations. At the same time, climate change and a need to transition from fossil fuels to renewable forms of energy are posing new challenges to the Dutch landscape. As such, contemporary ideas of maakbaarheid combine cross-scalar design strategies with social innovation in order to find new ways in which human and material resources can be redistributed to shape more sustainable environments (Brass *et al*. 2010).

3. EMERGING LANDSCAPES

The preceding paragraphs describe the social, environmental and economic conditions that helped inform the Dutch polder model and the idea of maakbaarheid. Key *modus operandi* underpinning both these frameworks are still very much alive in contemporary (landscape) design practices. In the face of current challenges related to urbanization, space limitations, rising sea levels, food and energy security, and economic uncertainty, a number of new design frameworks and approaches are emerging in the Netherlands. These approaches can be loosely divided into three categories: 1)*strategic interventions* marked by creative problem-solving, social engagement and resourcefulness; 2)proposals focusing on *urban metabolism* by reconfiguring flows of water, waste, energy and materials; 3)projects that envision new *climate change adaptation strategies*. What characterizes all these projects is that they are at once pragmatic and progressive, generating solutions to actual and future challenges. The remainder of this essay will explore these approaches and describe how they contribute to new ways of conceiving the built environment.

3.1. Strategic Interventions

In a time of limited budgets and finite resources, design practices have to develop alternative ways to get commissions and to implement projects. Whether through initiating community-based partnerships, crowd-funding or unsolicited proposals, in recent years designers have fostered exciting new funding models in order to turn ideas into real projects. These projects often include extensive social engagement and innovative ways to repurpose currently underutilized spaces and resources. Rather than starting from scratch, these projects involve *strategic interventions* that make deliberate use of urban resources and qualities that are already present in order to construct new contexts. Landscape architect Ronald Rietveld has defined strategic interventions as "precisely chosen and carefully designed urban or landscape interventions that set desired developments in motion" (Rietveld 2010). This idea is exemplified in the projects of the offices of DELVA landscape architects and LOLA landscape architects.

For example, DELVA was part of an interdisciplinary team that designed a soil cleaning and self-sufficient landscape featuring retrofitted houseboats, which now serve as offices, ateliers and workshops for creative and social enterprises. Located in Amsterdam, this project known as *De Ceuvel (2013)* incorporates an innovative temporary use strategy by turning 'wasted' land and materials into a valuable and productive urban space (Fig. 1). Guided by outcomes of a community-driven process, the idea is to occupy the site for a 10-year period while providing a demonstration site to test new clean technologies and environmental systems. The landscape not only creates an attractive aesthetic environment, it simultaneously purifies the soil, recycles nutrients, provides habitat, and produces biomass for the generation of energy to be used on-site. After 10 years, the boats can be easily moved to another location, while the land will be less polluted and more valuable, with a greater biodiversity.

Strategic interventions can also be implemented at a larger scale, as demonstrated by the proposal *Ecological Energy Network (2012)* of LOLA landscape architects, FABRIC and Studio 1:1. The proposal takes advantage of the easement and space underneath electricity grids in order to reconnect fragmented habitats, provide new types of green space and accommodate opportunities for leisure and recreation. Emphasizing the corridor's potential ecological significance, the design team envisions *Ecological Energy Network* as "the country's largest national park" by connecting existing parks while at the same time creating new ones (LOLA 2012). The project responds to "a craving for a new kind of landscape experience, and a romantic longing for nature…A wish of city folk to experience birds, bees, flowers, trees and wildlife from up close" (Bridger 2013). This is echoed by landscape architect Paul Roncken, who states that these types of projects recognize that "the sublime aspects of nature experiences nurture a sense of primordial survival and essential human capacity to creatively deal with the realistic conditions on Planet Landscape" (Rocken 2013: 148). Currently, the project team is establishing strategic partnerships with energy companies, provinces, and municipalities to implement the first kilometre of the Ecological Energy network in Eindhoven. By engaging different user groups, the goal is to define local opportunities for recreation and habitat development as well as to instil a sense of ownership and belonging to the space, which will help with the implementation and long-term maintenance of the project.

Fig.1. De Ceuvel as an innovative temporary use strategy (© DELVA Landscape Architects).

3.2. Urban Metabolism

Whereas strategic interventions are opportunistic and informed by specific site conditions, the concept of *urban metabolism* asks designers to analyse, comprehend and manipulate the flows of various resources, services and goods at the scale of the city and beyond. Following Abel Wolman's work *The Metabolism of Cities* (1965), this concept has been further developed in the fields of urban geography and urban political ecology (Kennedy et al. 2007). Within the context of design, contemporary spatial practices are increasingly interested in the following questions: How does urban metabolism work and how do materials flow through the city? What are the local implications of these flows of water, waste, energy, food and mobility? How can we recalibrate these flows individually, and as a system, to create positive social, ecological and economic changes in the built environment? (IABR 2014). In order to answer these questions, new analysis and research by design methods are emerging with particular emphasis on indexing and visualization of existing resource flows in the city. As argued by landscape architect James Corner, mapping is critical to any design process because it "allows for an understanding of terrain as only the surface expression of a complex and dynamic imbroglio of social and natural processes" (Corner 1999: 214). As such, mapping can help reveal geographic proximities, currently discarded resources and latent opportunities already existing in the landscape. Once visualized, spatial design can shape new conditions for combining flows and improving the way they relate to each other to create social, economic and ecological spin-offs.

The work of LINT landscape architects attempts this. Their speculative proposal *Dredge Landscape Park* (2006), utilizes 12 million cubic metres of polluted dredge that would otherwise be stored in costly confined disposal facilities. With climate change and increased pressures on land in the Netherlands, it will be important to find alternative ways to deal with this polluted dredge. As such, LINT proposes to collect, separate and clean polluted dredge by a carefully calibrated landscape system. Salt water (from the North Sea) is used to clean different types of pollution in the dredge: heavy metals, organic pollution and a mixture of both. Since each of the cleaning processes takes place at different locations and involving different material inputs, over time, a unique landscape emerges that includes a metal garden, a strip of artificial dunes and a mosaic of different water, soil and vegetation types (Fig. 2). Envisioned as a landscape machine, the design combines the logic of agricultural systems (based on mechanical inputs and productivity) with ecological processes (based on dynamic interactions and emergence) to create a resilient framework (Roncken *et al.* 2011). Excess cleaned sand can be sold and used in nearby development project, generating income to fund park operations and maintenance. Moreover, the proposal promotes a new kind of aesthetic: an ever-changing landscape that is operational while also generating emergent conditions for various types of biotopes.

A similar interest in urban metabolism informs the *IABR-Project Atelier Rotterdam* (2014), a collaborative between the City of Rotterdam, Dutch design firm FABRIC and James Corner Field Operation (United States). As one of the first holistic research by design projects focusing on the metabolism of an entire city, the project mapped and visualized nine different flows vital to the economy and ecology of Rotterdam: goods, people, waste, biota, energy, food, fresh water, air, sand and clay. After extensive analysis of these flows, the design team developed various urban design strategies in order to create synergies between on-going and future developments, to optimize recovery and reuse of (raw) materials, to reduce the impacts on the environment, and to improve the quality of life (IABR 2014). Waste management, for example, can be redesigned to create benefits for residents as well as the urban region as a whole (IABR 2014). On the community level, this might entail the establishment of 'protein collectives' and small-scale biogas plants that utilize organic household waste and human faeces as a source of nutrient-rich fertilizer for urban farming. On a regional scale, by-products of industrial processes, such as excess heat can be redirected to local district heating network or used for the generation of energy. Similarly, CO_2 can be captured, transported and used in nearby greenhouses to boost agriculture and limit CO_2 emissions

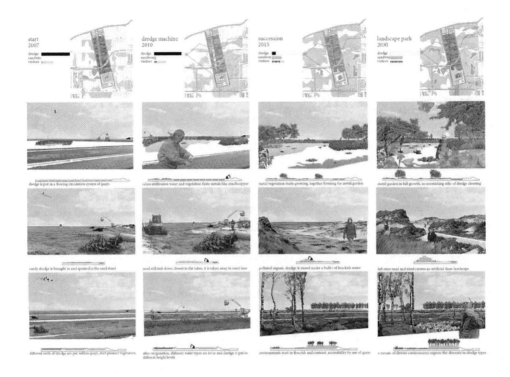

Fig.2. Dredge Landscape Park (© LINT Landscape Architects).

(IABR 2014). *Project Atelier Rotterdam* recognizes that these flows will change in quantity and location in the future, and that continuous cross-scalar design strategies are necessary to ensure sustainable conditions. The project team suggests that "designing the city on the basis of its urban metabolism requires shifting between regional and local scales; between strategic design and spatial design; between flows and the associated infrastructure" (IABR 2014: 141). Beyond developing new planning and design methods, this also necessitates the establishment of new public-private partnerships involving residents, neighbourhood groups, the private sectors and city departments.

3.3. Climate Proofing

In addition to growing interests in urban metabolism and resource optimization, climate change presents another concrete challenge informing contemporary spatial design practices in the Netherlands. Whereas rising sea levels will immediately impact over a quarter of the country that is located below sea level, climate change will also result in an increased frequency and severity of extreme weather events. This means the likelihood of flash flooding events, enhanced river-flows and potential droughts is to increase as well, which will affect urban areas, agriculture and ecosystems. In this context, I will discuss two projects; one related to integrated water management on a regional scale and another concerning the potential for small-scale climate change adaptation strategies.

While the Dutch have a state of the art flood control system (designed and implemented after the flood of 1953), in recent decades, planners, designers and decision-makers have been exploring new ways of water management that are less informed by notions of control but instead work *with* water (Rijke *et al.* 2012). It took floods in 1993 and 1995—for the latter nearly 250,000 people and 1 million cattle were evacuated—to create public awareness and for the Dutch government to form an adhoc committee (the *Room for the River Directive)* to frame new policies and guidelines related to water management. The aim of this Directive was to establish how water could be envisioned as a key structuring principles for spatial development in the Netherlands. The Dutch Senate eventually approved its recommendations in 2006 (Rijke et al. 2012). At a cost of the 2.2 billion Euro, the *Room for the River* program has two main goals: 1) to accommodate a discharge capacity of 16,000 m3/s in the floodplains of the Rivers Rhine, Meuse, Waal, IJssel and Lek, and; 2) to improve the spatial and ecological quality of the areas along these rivers (Rijke *et al.* 2012). Rather than one mega-project, the program consists of 39 distinct but interconnected projects in order to meet these goals. Together, the projects combine a variety of strategies, including flood bypasses, dike setbacks and relocations, excavation of flood plains and removal of any obstacles. Various leading water research institutes helped with the development of a digital hydrologic model to calculate, coordinate and assess the overall effectiveness of all 39 projects.

Among the more visible sub-projects is *Ruimte voor de Waal*, which consists of the implementation of a new bypass channel at Nijmegen and Lent (Fig. 3). This intervention not only increases flood storage but it also creates a new island and unique setting for new recreation and ecological restoration. Combining new models of flood management with enhanced spatial development, this project has received numerous recognitions, including the International Waterfront Award (2011) and Red Dot Public Space Award (2011) for innovative community engagement and participation strategies (Nijssen and Schouten 2012). Jeroen Rijke *et al.* have argued that, "through application of a mixed centralized–decentralized governance approach, the programme has tackled governance pitfalls related to centralized planning approaches that previously impeded integrated water management" (Rijke *et al.* 2012: 379).

At the neighbourhood scale, Dutch spatial practices are also at the forefront of developing progressive climate change adaptation strategies. With *Water Square Benthemplein* (2013), Rotterdam recently welcomed a new addition to their portfolio of public spaces. Designed by the Dutch firm De Urbanisten, the water square combines innovative stormwater management with the introduction of a multifunctional public space. The square features various planting areas surrounding a sunken plaza with basins at

Fig.3. Ruimte voor de Waal (© Johan Roerink/Aeropicture).

Fig.4. Rotterdam Water Square (© De Urbanisten).

different depths. During dry weather the space can be used for various leisure and recreational activities but in times of heavy rain, the basins can be temporarily submerged in order to relieve Rotterdam's sewage system. Water is collected from adjacent rooftops and impervious surfaces and transported via oversized steel gutters before it enters the basins. After rain events, water from the deepest basin is released into the stormwater system of the city. Water of the two other basins is redirected into an underground infiltration device that recharges the groundwater (De Urbanisten 2011). In addition to providing a highly visible and sustainable model for rethinking urban water management, the design team also facilitated an extensive community engagement process to receive input, and collaborate, on the form and function of the square. As such, many have praised the water square for "its innovative character, but also its multi-actor cooperation, its work on the boundaries between short term and long term effects, and its multi-domain and multi-objective focus" (Bressers and Edelenbos 2014: 88).

4. CONCLUSIONS

As a small, densely populated country partially situated below sea level, the Dutch have a long history of manipulating the physical landscape in order to respond to evolving social, economic and environmental issues. Currently, the challenges of economic uncertainty, growing resource scarcity, energy transitions, and climate change, are providing new necessities and motivations for design innovation. This essay has foregrounded emerging Dutch landscape design practices that fundamentally engages these challenges. From the re-appropriation of 'wasted' spaces and resources, to recalibrating the urban metabolism of entire cities, to progressive climate change adaptation strategies, the projects discussed envision radically new relationships between people and their spatial environment. Since the issues these projects are trying to tackle are relevant in many places around the world, so may the design methods and approaches they have developed and implemented. We can already see proof of this in the realm of integrated water management. Recent initiatives such as *Dutch Dialogues* (New Orleans) and *Rebuild by Design* (New York), for example, are explicitly integrating Dutch design expertise. Similar efforts are also underway in countries such as Vietnam, Bangladesh and Indonesia (Kabat *et al.* 2013).

Moreover, Dredge Landscape Park and Project Atelier Rotterdam provide initial ideas of how design practices have the capacity to link regional processes to local opportunities in order to create multiple benefits. As populations globally are increasingly living in urbanized regions, there is a need to test how the urban metabolism philosophy can optimize where we get our resources from, and how various waste-streams can inform new urban developments.

Finally, in addition to the actual design strategies presented in this paper, there is something to learn from the way in which local and national (government) initiatives enable the development of progressive design practices in the Netherlands. The proposal for Ecological Energy Network, for example, was part of an initiative initiated by the Netherlands Architecture Institute and the Dutch ministry of Economic Affairs, Agriculture and Innovation. This platform provided funding for a select number of proposals in order to enable designers to create alliances with potential stakeholders. Similarly, there are dozens of other initiatives that provide designers opportunities (often through seed-funding) to develop proposal for which there currently might not be specific clients. Taken together, it is the combination of a contested landscape, and public support that enables a new generation of designers in the Netherlands to explore progressive solutions for pressing socio-spatial and environmental conditions.

BIBLIOGRAPHY

Bressers, N., and Edelenbos, J. (2014). Planning for adaptivity: Facing complexity in innovative urban water squares. *Emergence: Complexity and Organization*, 16(1), pp. 77-99.

Corner, J. (1999). The agency of mapping: Speculation, critique and invention. In: D. Cosgrove, ed., *Mappings*. London: Reakton Books, pp. 214-252.

De Ceuvel (2013). *Cleantech playground.* [online] Available at: http://deceuvel.nl [access 8 February 2016].

De Urbanisten (2011). *Water square Benthemplein.* [online] Available at: http://www.urbanisten.nl/wp/?portfolio=waterplein-benthemplein [access 10 February 2016].

de Vries, J. (2014). The Netherlands and the polder model: Questioning the polder model concept. *Bmgn-the Low Countries Historical Review*, 129(1), pp. 99-111.

Declerck, J., and Vande Velde, D. (2005). After the party. *OASE Magazine* Nr. 67, pp. 112-120.

Kabat, P., Zevenbergen, C., Herk, S. and Rijke, J. (2013). Taming global flood disasters. Lessons learned from Dutch experience. *Natural Hazards*, 65(3), pp. 1217-1225.

Kennedy, C., Cuddihy, J. and Engel-Yan, J. (2007). The changing metabolism of cities. *Journal of Industrial Ecology*, 11(2), pp. 43-59.

LINT Landscape Architecture (2007). Dredge landscape park. online] Available at: http://landscapeinterventions.nl/en/dredge-landscape-park [access 12 February 2016].

LOLA Landscape Architects (2012). Ecological Energy Network. [online] Available at: http://www.lolaweb.nl/projecten.php?id=70 [access 11 February 2016].

Lootsma, B. (2000). *Super-Dutch: New architecture in the Netherlands.* London: Thames & Hudson.

Nijssen, P. and Schouten M. (2012) Dutch national Room for the River project: Integrated approach for river safety and urban development. *1st IS.Rivers Conference*, 26-28 June 2012, Lyon, France. [online] Available at: http://www.graie.org/ISRivers/actes/pdf2012/1A108-265NIJ.pdf [access 11 January, 2016].

Rijke, J., van Herk, S., Zevenbergen, C. and Ashley, R. (2012). Room for the river: Delivering integrated river basin management in the Netherlands. *International Journal of River Basin Management,* 10(4), pp. 369-382.

Roncken, P. A., (2013). Lost landscapes. In: Veeken, C. v. d., Meindertsma, E., & Veenstra, A. ed., *Lost landscapes: LOLA landscape architects*. Rotterdam: Nai010 Publishers, pp. 146-151.

Roncken, P. A., Stremke, S. and Paulissen, Maurice P. C. P. (2011). Landscape machines: Productive nature and the future sublime. *Journal of Landscape Architecture,* 6(1), pp. 68-81.

Salewski, C. (2012). *Dutch new worlds: Scenarios in physical planning and design in the Netherlands, 1970-2000.* Rotterdam: 010 Publishers.

Schuilenburg, M. (2015). *The securitization of society: Crime, risk, and social order.* NYU Press.

The 4th International Architecture Biennale Rotterdam (2009). *Open city: Designing coexistence.* [online] Available at: http://iabr.nl/media/document/original/catalog_4thiabr_en.pdf [access 15 February 2016].

The International Architecture Biennale Rotterdam (2014). *Urban metabolism: sustainable development Rotterdam.* [online] Available at: http://iabr.nl/urban_metabolism_rotterdam.pdf [access 16 February 2016].

van 't Klooster, I. (2013). *Reactivate!: Innovators of Dutch Architecture.* Amsterdam: Valiz/Trancity.

van Tielhof, M. (2015). Forced solidarity: Maintenance of coastal defences along the North Sea coast in the early modern period. *Environment and History*, 21(3), pp. 319-350.

Vanstiphout, W. (2006). *Dirty minimalism: The liberation of unimportance in recent Dutch architecture.* Harvard Design Magazine, (24).

Vanstiphout, W. and Proovoost, M. (2009). Maakbaarheid. Reinventing the urban project in Rotterdam. In: T.Rieniets, J.Sigler, K. and Christiaanse, K. eds., *Open city: designing coexistence.* Amsterdam: SUN, pp. 417-456.

EXPERIENCING LANDSCAPE.
A PHENOMENOLOGICAL PERSPECTIVE

Carlo Guareschi
University College Cork

ABSTRACT

In this paper, I draw on a possible conception of landscape from Merleau-Ponty's philosophy. Starting from an overview of the two main positions regarding landscape within the continental philosophical tradition (Simmel and Ritter), I consider the use of the term 'landscape' in Merleau-Ponty's thought, without wishing to claim that the French philosopher presents a philosophy of landscape within his works. I want to show that important elements for the outline of a phenomenological conception of landscape emerge from Merleau-Ponty's philosophy. According to Simmel, landscape is seen as the product of a spiritual act, and in Ritter's perspective, landscape emerges from a detached contemplation of nature proper to humans in the modern era. Contrasted with these views, a consideration of Merleau-Ponty's original works allows to draw on a conception of landscape in which the experiential and perceptual dimensions are fundamental. This view enables us to consider landscape in its centrality for human experience, and leads to a better understanding of the strong ontological commitment between humans and nature.

Keywords
Landscape, Experience, Aesthetics, Phenomenology, Merleau-Ponty

1. INTRODUCTION

Landscape represents an interesting issue for a philosophical investigation. From a theoretical point of view, landscape is a complex object in which culture and nature interact; from an aesthetical point of view, landscape displays specific perceptual features that interact with our own appreciation of the wider realm of nature. In the last decades, and with the increase of environmental problems, the necessity of rethinking our experience of nature and its preservation has emerged. This debate plays a pivotal role within environmental philosophy and environmental aesthetics, aestheticians and philosophers, such as Aldo Leopold, Allen Carlson, Arnold Berleant, Edward S. Casey and Ted Toadvine among others, started from different perspectives to investigate our modalities of natural appreciation. If it is true that a reflection concerning our natural experience is present in the history of philosophy, it is equally true that after Kant, and specifically with the advent of Hegelian philosophy and its hyper-evaluation of Spiritual activity, nature as an object of investigation almost disappeared from the aesthetical debate. However, it is possible to find one exception in the phenomenology of Maurice Merleau-Ponty, as I shall discuss in the present paper.

2. CONTENTS

Before trying to provide a phenomenological account of landscape, a step back is necessary. All philological research converges on the fact that the word "landscape" (*landschap*) has indicated, between the 15th and 16th Centuries, both the pictorial representation of a portion of the territory connoted by aesthetic values, and the territory in its concrete physical reality (morphological structure), though such research still maintains a certain ambivalence. Despite this ambivalence, the term was especially used in the first sense and was understood as the pictorial representation of a certain portion of the territory. As such, the landscape began to be experienced as an image. After this preliminary philological and historical consideration, it is important to notice that within contemporary continental philosophy there are two main relevant positions. One is provided by Georg Simmel (2007) in his famous essay *Philosophy of Landscape*, the other one is presented by Joachim Ritter (2001) in his work *Landscape. Man and Nature in the Modern Era*. For Simmel, the emergence of a landscape is due to a twofold reason. Firstly, the constitution of a landscape emerges immediately through the visual delimitation borne out of the impression of the singular things of nature that are successively constituted into a unity. On a second level, landscape emerges as an artistic work, which has to be understood as an 'intensification' of what happens at the previous level. The simmelian analysis assumes that the artistic categories are still in action in the common formation of a landscape that is subsequently brought to fulfillment, or sublimated by the artistic act. Therefore, the norms that guide the realization of the landscape can be understood in parallelism to the normativity activity displayed in the creation of an artwork. After this cross-referenced consideration, Simmel introduces the fundamental concept of *Stimmung* (translated with the English term 'mood'):

"We say that a landscape arises when a range of natural phenomena spread over the surface of the earth is comprehended by a particular kind of unity, one that is distinct from the way this same visual field is encompassed by the causally thinking scholar, the religious sentiments of a worshipper of nature, the teleologically oriented tiller of the soil, or a strategist of war. The most important carrier of this unity may well be the 'mood', as we call it, of a landscape" (Simmel 2007: 26).

What constitutes the mood of a landscape is a 'psychic act' that composes this specific segment of the natural continuum in a specific unity. It seems that the simmelian perspective oscillates between subjectivism ('psychic act') and objectivism ('mood'). It remains obscure how it is possible to conceive this aesthetic object in its own mood when it is clear that it is derived from the artistic activity of an individual. It becomes possible to highlight two orders of problems: firstly, the tension between subjectivity and objectivity of the mood of landscape is unsolved. Second, the artist is the responsible for the constitution of a certain landscape: how, then, is it possible for the artist to create a concrete landscape if (for Simmel) the landscape is not a picture but a segment of nature as a whole? The problem of the constitution of a landscape is addressed from a different perspective in Joachim Ritter. If Simmel focused the analysis on the artistic or spiritual act of creation, Ritter found the genesis of landscape within modernity. For Ritter, landscape arises from a separation between humans and nature; with the increasing growth of urbanization, the free contemplation of nature became an element external to the daily life. The experience of landscape became possible only when humans began to have a detached relationship with the natural element. Furthermore, for Ritter the perceptive dimension of this detached aesthetic experience claims universality, and in doing so is closer to theoretical activity. Starting from this point of view, aesthetical experience appears to be complementary to natural science. Landscape is important because it allows us to re-evaluate a conception of nature related to intuition and experience, it requires an aesthetic conception which is excluded from natural science. The meaningful aspect of Ritter's analysis is to suggest the centrality and universality of aesthetic experience.

Both these positions provide important elements that could aid in formulating a phenomenological account of landscape. From Simmel we can develop the concept of *Stimmung* and from Ritter we can draw on the centrality of intuition and the aesthetic experience. However, how is it possible to provide a phenomenological synthesis of this two element? Dealing in phenomenological terms with this question requires us to consider the qualitative aspect of our experience of landscape. As Casey suggests (2007), landscape is what allows the place-world to appear and, in being characterized by its layout and surface(1), it could be considered expressive in itself. This connection between surface and expressivity appears to be central in order to try to provide an account of landscape in which the central element is its experiential dimension.

In this paper, the aim is not to argue that Merleau-Ponty provides a philosophy of landscape. This would be fruitless because in Merleau-Ponty's philosophy it is impossible to find any explicit analysis of landscape at all. Nonetheless, in some interesting passages in his *Phenomenology of Perception* and *The Visible and the Invisible*, he presents interesting stimuli for re-thinking our conception of landscape. In particular, Merleau-Ponty's phenomenology allows us to concentrate an analysis on the experiential dimension of landscape. Previously it has been shown that within the classical position in continental philosophy there is a tension between subject and landscape, man and nature. At the same time, Casey recently pointed out how it is possible to link surface (the perceptual features of a landscape) with expressivity of landscapes. In what follows I want show how, starting from Merleau-Ponty's phenomenology, it is possible to overcome a dualistic consideration of the relationship between landscape and subjectivity. This implies an enlargement of the conception of landscape because it assumes that landscape configures itself not only as a manifestation of the place-world, but furthermore as an experiential dimension of our aesthetic experience *tout court*.

I want start the consideration with a brief presentation of Merleau-Ponty's analysis of Cézanne. Merleau-Ponty provides an interpretation of Cézanne in his article *Cézanne's Doubt*[2], and clearly shows how, for him, the painting activity of Cézanne is devoted to an obsessive research of the nonhuman world. This inexhaustible research appears in Cézanne's studying of landscape, in his constant investment in dialectic knowledge and forgiveness, knowledge and pre-categorial experience. His aim was to capture the co-emerging of a landscape from nature, or, more generally, the co-emerging of humanity and non-humanity:

"Motivating all the movements from which a picture gradually emerges there can be only one thing: the landscape in its totality and in its absolute fullness, precisely what Cezanne called a 'motif'. He would start by discovering the geological foundations of the landscape; then, according to Madame Cezanne, he would halt and look at everything with widened eyes, "germinating" with the countryside. The task before him was, first, to forget all he had ever learned from science and, second, through these sciences to recapture the structure of the landscape as an emerging organism" (Merleau-Ponty 2007: 76-77).

This obsession for nature and brute being is central in Merleau-Ponty's investigations and specifically in his rethinking the possibility and limits of phenomenology itself. Cézanne's struggle to capture the emergence of being completely resembles the merleau-pontian investigation of the primordial world of perceptive experience. This focusing on landscape represents the tangible sign of a deeper interest in our participation to nature. It thus appears clear that for Merleau-Ponty landscape is, as with Cézanne, the concrete element of interaction between subjectivity and nature. It is not surprising that Merleau-Ponty uses landscape to express his conception of perception. Initially, landscape appears to be the visible exemplum of the dialectic between pre-categorical and categorical activity, between mute and wild being and thematized being. Furthermore, landscape in its visible displaying of invisible features becomes the concrete place to consider the effectiveness of the eidetic reduction.

It is in the *Phenomenology of Perception* that Merleau-Ponty provides his account on perception and lived body. It is not my aim here to offer a complete analysis of his complex work, but rather, to consider a few passages in which landscape appears to be central in his considerations. At the beginning of his chapter *The phenomenal field*, Merleau-Ponty is critically analyzing the concept of pure quale, the idea of the existence of a pure *datum* of perception. If starting from the idea of an impartial mind this idea might be plausible, then on the other hand, according to a phenomenological analysis of the bodily subjectivity, it is impossible to find this purity. According to his re-consideration of the concept of Ego, sensation is understood in its richness of connections. It is specifically in his consideration of the strong relationship between sensation and body that Merleau-Ponty introduce landscape:

"The problem is to understand these strange relations woven between the parts of the landscape, or from the landscape to me as an embodied subject, relations by which a perceived object can condense within itself an entire scene or become the imago of an entire segment of life. Sensing is this living communication with the world that makes it present to us as the familiar place of our life. The perceived object and the perceiving subject owe their thickness to sensing" (Merleau-Ponty 2012: 53).

It appears clear that landscape is central in virtue of its being a concrete experiential object. In addition, landscape require the presence of the subject as an embodied subjectivity who is able to sense. This sensation, rather than be the pure content of any intentional activity, appears to be the anchor to the concrete world. Furthermore, in connecting landscape with the question of invisible features, this lived object 'condenses' in itself the 'imago of an entire segment of live'. This means, in other words, that landscape in its strong connection with our experience displays not only sensible features (such as colors, smells, a certain conformation of the vegetation and so on) but also the concrete possibility of our spatial and temporal protentions. It appears clear that in Merleau-Ponty's view landscape is more than just a simple object. It is not surprising that Merleau-Ponty deepened the analysis of spatiality in connection with bodily experience and it is within these considerations that the term landscape appears again. Before considering this step forward, it is necessary to focus more on the perceptual dimension of landscape. Firstly, for Merleau-Ponty landscape is a connection of parts. Secondly, landscape implies subjectivity in its bodily presence. This interconnection is made possible by the activity of sensing, which plays an important role in Merleau-Ponty's phenomenology(2). At this stage, we can find three important elements that appear to be central in our experience of landscape: sensing/perception, spatiality and body. In fact, starting from this example of landscape, Merleau-Ponty starts to structure his reconsideration of the transcendental field and Ego as bodily presence and reflection. This triad allows Merleau-Ponty to consider meaningful issues of spatiality, specifically the intersection between body and the primordial level of spatiality, which develops to a higher level a dialectic between history and pre-history. This is a pivotal issue in Merleau-Ponty's analysis because it expresses his conviction of the necessity of a phenomenological consideration of the primordial world of experience, a layer antecedent to any thought. The issue of spatiality is complex and it is dealt with throughout the merleau-pontian works: to summarize and to contextualize it to the present aim, I want to focus the analysis on few dense pages in the *Phenomenology of Perception*, where the term 'landscape' re-appears.

In the paragraph, *Being has sense only through its orientation* (3), Merleau-Ponty analyzes the fundamental connection between bodily perception and spatiality. To put it in other words, Merleau-Ponty is considering the possible interaction of different layers in our participation to the world. The merleau-pontian analysis of this primordial space consists of three passages. Firstly, "the constitution of a level always presupposes another given level, that space always precedes itself" (Merleau-Ponty 2012: 262). Space is a constant element in our experience, and furthermore, it delineates our coordinates of bodily experience. Secondly, "the primordial level is on the horizon of all of our perceptions, but this is a horizon that, in principle, can never be reached and thematized in an explicit perception" (Merleau-Ponty 2012: 262). It appears that there is a connection between the primordial level and the horizon of our perception, but it is hard to define clearly this relationship and the difference between the primordial level and this horizon. This requires a further analysis that cannot be done in this context. Nonetheless, what emerges here is that this spatiality is something extremely dynamic that puts us in constant and always richer layers of experience. Thirdly, "my first perception and my first hold on the world must appear to me as the execution of a more ancient pact established between x and the world in general; my history must be the sequel to a pre-history whose acquired results it uses; my personal existence must be the taking up of a pre-personal tradition" (Merleau-Ponty 2012: 265). Merleau-Ponty started from the ontological correlation between body and world, then proceeded to the consideration of spatiality, and finally arrived at a higher layer of sedimentation within the subjectivity in which space structures the dynamic relationship between history and pre-history. According to what has been shown, what emerges is that the dialectic between the primordial level and the horizon of possible perceptions functions as a basis for the higher dialectic between nature and culture. This point is central because it is this constant actualization and enrichment of the past perceptions that facilitates the emergence of the culture (history) within nature (pre-history).

It is exactly in starting from this higher level in the dialectic of spatiality that Merleau-Ponty clarifies what constitutes the main element for him. Once again, in order to explain his point of view, Merleau-Ponty introduces the term landscape:

"The positing of a level is the forgetting of this contingency, and space is established upon our facticity. Space in neither an object, nor an act of connecting by the subject: one can neither observe it (given that it is presupposed in every observation), nor see it emerging from a constitutive operation (given that it is of its essence to be already constituted); and this is how it can magically bestow upon the landscape its spatial determinations without itself ever appearing" (Merleau-Ponty 2012: 265).

Space is already there, it is at the core of our presence in the world. Merleau-Ponty is proposing a conception of lived space according to which it becomes impossible to grasp the eidetic structure of space in an act of thematization. It seems that for Merleau-Ponty the intuitive affordance of space is something basilar, something constitutive of our experience *tout court*. Space is thematized in the pure sciences and then becomes object of theoretical investigation, but it is nonetheless possible to investigate its primordial dimension starting from the intuitive experience that we have before any doxic thematization. Landscape appears to be the concrete place in which we participate in the emergence of spatiality; landscape as *sui generis* experience allows us to rethink the connections between categorical and pre-categorical, history and pre-history, nature and culture. I use the term 'experience' rather than the term 'object' in order to stress the experiential dimension of landscape. In accordance with this experiential line of interpretation of landscape, it is possible to attempt to provide an alternative to the dichotomous perspectives provided by Simmel and Ritter. According to what I have previously shown, on the one hand Simmel presents a perspective in which landscape appears to be a product of spiritual activity. On the other hand, Ritter highlights how landscape emerges within a detached experience of nature. These perspectives are tied to a classical conception that reduces landscape to a mere object of contemplation. However, it becomes possible to extrapolate two elements from Simmel and Ritter and then interwoven each other in a different ground. Firstly, it is necessary to consider the concept of *Stimmung* taken from Simmel's *Philosophy of Landscape*. On the one hand, the 'mood' is what characterizes the action of unification of different elements in one singular landscape. On the other hand, a certain mood is what distinguishes this specific landscape as such. As Simmel points out: "could it not be that the mood of a landscape and the perceptual unity of a landscape are one and the same thing, only viewed from two different angles, both one and the same means that can be expressed in a dual way, through which a beholder brings about a landscape, this particular landscape, out of adjoining pieces?" (Simmel 2007: 27). It is exactly regarding this difficulty that it becomes useful to integrate the concept of *Stimmung* with a genetic interpretation of spatiality, as Merleau-Ponty did.

In considering what Merleau-Ponty claimed concerning our fundamental bodily correlation with the world, what clearly emerges is that the mood of the landscape is a correlative element that in its expressive function connects subject and landscape. The mood is something in-between that brings to light the fundamental connection and coincidence amongst expression (mood) and expressed (the encountering between a certain place and me). For example, a certain landscape appears to be ominous or sad in virtue of the encounter between its structure and my experience. If I am lost in the wood in a cold winter night, with a high full moon, I will probably perceive my being in this specific landscape as ominous. Most probably other people, even not all, will perceive the same 'ominosity' in the same situation. What is interesting is that this mood is a question of experience, experience that connects precisely the being of a landscape as such with my bodily presence here and now. It is not a mere projection of the subjectivity in a natural composition but my experiencing of landscape in a certain situation that allows me to appreciate that peculiar mood. At this point, it can be asked if this restlessness is properly representative of mere subjectivity. It seems that the answer should be no, because this mood is experienced in very specific context. Another question thereby raises: is it then this restlessness that is a property of the landscape in itself? I think the answer is negative in this direction also. Holding that a landscape is landscape-in-itself draws the objection of significant anthropomorphism. One problem, for example, will be to clarify how we know that landscape is ominous in itself. Is the landscape self-aware of its being-restless? How can we attribute to landscape the ability to perceive itself as a landscape? I would suggest that it may be possible to overcome these problems if we assume that, in the case of landscape, a mood is a relational experience. If we try to consider this correlational condition implied in our experience of landscape, it also becomes possible to integrate it with Ritter's claim that we need an aesthetically mediated truth. However, if for Ritter aesthetics aims at universality, then it is possible in its being detached contemplation. On the contrary, according to Merleau-Ponty's phenomenology aesthetics appears to be the core of our embodied experience. The centrality of bodily and lived experience brings the analysis to another interesting passage in which Merleau-Ponty introduces again the term 'landscape'. In the paragraph of the *Phenomenology of Perception* entitled *Lived space*, Merleau-Ponty provides an interesting analysis of schizophrenia in relation to lived spatiality. Before specifying the connection between experience of landscape and pathology, Merleau-Ponty clarifies his conception of landscape, "our body and our perception always solicit us to take the landscape they offer as the center of the world. But this landscape is not necessarily the landscape of our life. I can 'be elsewhere' while remaining here" (Merleau-Ponty 2012: 299).

It is necessary to highlight two elements from this quote. Firstly, landscape configures itself as an experience framed by the activity of our perceptual body. Secondly, landscape appears to be a constant framing of different spatial locations, it does not exhaust the complexity of life from a single point of view. Merleau-Ponty stresses clearly that from my local position, namely my current landscape, I can operate a variation which allows my 'being elsewhere while remaining here'. This point is important because it is according to this variation – that could be imaginative or spatial – that landscape is not a single and total possession of a certain portion of space by the subject, but rather is a continuous synthesis of different experience. It is precisely in relation to this relationship between two different kinds of spatiality, between visible and invisible, that Merleau-Ponty introduces the case of schizophrenia. Merleau-Ponty stresses how, within it, the intersubjective space is penetrated also "by another spatiality that morbid variations reveal" (Merleau-Ponty: 2012: 300). In the case of the schizophrenic, this space permeates the normal space in a decisive way and alters completely the perception of the normal landscape. As Merleau-Ponty points out:

"The schizophrenic patient no longer lives in the common world, but in a private world; he does not go all the way to geographical space, he remains within 'the space of the landscape' (3), and this landscape itself, once cut off from the common world, is considerably impoverished" (Merleau-Ponty 2012: 300).

It emerges clearly that for Merleau-Ponty landscape is not a mere object but rather an experience related to the *hic et nunc* of our bodily experience. In this example of schizophrenia, it appears clearly that landscape is the concrete display of my perceptual and emotional experience of space that is fundamentally related to the intersubjective world. In cutting off his own landscape, the schizophrenic experiences the "second space" as an absolute. Then, if landscape appears to be a framing of lived space according with our perceptive and psychical structure, then it is possible to assume that landscape is a natural display of our living the world as an embodied subjects. Furthermore, landscape emerges as the place in which we are constantly re-framing and synthetizing our spatiality. As Merleau-Ponty marvelously wrote in *The Visible and the Invisible*:

"Each landscape of my life, because it is not a wandering troop of sensation or a system of ephemeral judgments but a segment of the durable flesh of the world, is qua visible, pregnant with many others visions besides my own. […] When I find again the actual world such as it is, under my hands, under my eyes, up against my body, I find much more than an object: a Being of which my vision is part, a visibility older than my operations or my acts" (Marleau-Ponty 1964: 123).

3. CONCLUSIONS

In the previous lines, I tried to provide an account of landscape starting from the phenomenology of Merleau-Ponty. In a preliminary manner, I highlighted the two dominant positions within continental philosophy, and I then introduced the phenomenological reading of landscape elaborated by Casey. Starting from this basis, I examined some passages in Merleau-Ponty's works in which landscape appears to be relevant. Even though it is impossible to provide here a complete account of the problem of landscape, I want point out that using Merleau-Ponty's phenomenology can broaden the concept of landscape and arrives at a conception that considers landscape in its experiential structure. I want to suggest that seeing landscape in its experiential dimension provides more radical ontological reasons to preserve it. Rather than considering it as an object of possible preservation, landscape as an experience becomes the concrete display of our experience of nature as humans and natural beings. Therefore, landscape does not appear only in its cultural or aesthetical values but also in its ontological primacy. This 'strong' conception of landscape demands a fundamental re-consideration of the centrality of our lived experience of nature.

NOTES

[1]   Casey provides an interesting consideration of landscape and provides a twofold characterization of its structure. Referring to Gibson's theory of affordances, Casey points out that "layout" is the visible structure of a place-world that indicates or 'provides opportunities to its inhabitants' (Casey 2007: 369). Casey specifies that this layout of a specific place-world or environment is a sequence of surfaces. It is exactly by these surfaces that we experience a certain environment. The analysis introduced by Casey is useful to deepen a merleau-pontian investigation of landscape, especially if we consider that Casey introduces for the surface a merleau-pontian concept proper of spatiality and body: expressivity. As Casey clearly points out: 'surfaces show themselves to be eminently capable of expressivity. [...] This is due to the fact that surfaces are capable of the kind of variation that are important to expressivity. I think here of variations in pliability, elasticity, contour, extendedness, coloration, texture, and so forth. [...] It is just because of this multiplicity of co-variant factors that the full range of expressivity is possible, whether it is displayed in a face or in the layout of a landscape' (Casey 2007: 371).

[2]   Merleau-Ponty, M. (1964). *Cézanne's doubt*, in Toadvine T., Lawlor L. (2007). *The Merleau-Ponty reader*. Evanston: Northwestern University Press.

[3]   (Merleau-Ponty 2012: 262).

[4]   For the sake of precision, it is necessary to highlight that starting from this relevance given to the sensuous dimension, Merleau-Ponty developed – especially in *The visible and Invisible* and in his course notes – relevant concepts such as "chiasm". This term stresses our ontological co-participation to the world, we are flesh and consequently the perceiving body is what locates us in the midst of the world. As Merleau-Ponty clearly explains in his famous chapter of *The visible and the Invisible* entitled *The Intertwining-The Chiasm*: "it is that the thickness of the flesh between the seer and the thing is constitutive for the thing of its visibility as for the seer of his corporeity; it is not an obstacle between them, it is their means of communication" (Merleau-Ponty 1968: 135).

[5]   Merleau-Ponty is quoting: (Straus 1935: 290).

BIBLIOGRAPHY

Casey, E. (2007). *The World at a Glance*. Bloomington: Indiana University Press.

Marleau-Ponty, M. (1964). *The Visible and the Invisible*. Evanston: Northwestern University Press.

Marleau-Ponty, M. (2012). *The Phenomenology of Perception*. London: Routledge.

Ritter, J. (2001). *Paesaggio. Uomo e Natura Nell'Età Moderna*. Milano, Guerini e Associati.

Simmel G. (2007). *Philosophy of Landscape*. Theory, Culture & Society 24(6).

Straus, E. (1935). *Vom Sinn der Sinne*. Berlin: Springer.

THE PHILOSOPHY OF LANDSCAPE. CONTEMPORARY PERSPECTIVES

Mateusz Salwa
University of Warsaw, Institute of Philosophy

ABSTRACT

The aim of the article is to offer an overview of contemporary philosophical approaches to the concept of landscape. Despite the fact that it is justified to treat landscapes as mainly aesthetic phenomena, it is erroneous to simply identify the philosophy of landscape with landscape aesthetics. Not only does such a reductive approach ignore certain issues (e.g. ethical ones), but it also is based on implicit assumptions as to what a landscape is. As a result, it does not raise the question "what is a landscape?" The philosophy of landscape instead is an attempt at solving this issue. In the article two general approaches are discussed. The first is the traditional one which treats landscapes as spectacular visual "objects" and the second is the phenomenological one which conceives of them as experienced dwelling places. Finally, a provisional definition of the landscape experience is given. The analyses are based on two legal documents that offer two divergent conceptions of landscape, i.e. the UNESCO World Heritage Convention (1992) and the European Landscape Convention (2000).

Keywords
aesthetics, landscape, philosophy

The first to coin the term "philosophy of landscape" was probably Simmel in 1913 (Simmel, 2007). Today it is not frequently used (D'Angelo 2009; Le Dantec 2006; Verríssimo and Serrão, 2013) ([1]), which is due to the fact that philosophical considerations of landscapes are dominated by aesthetic issues. As a consequence, the philosophy of landscape tends to be replaced by the aesthetics of landscape. Even though it is justified to treat the landscape as, above all, an aesthetic phenomenon (as it will be done below), it is erroneous to limit the philosophy of landscape only to landscape aesthetics as it results in a disregard for e.g. ethical issues (Donadieu 2012: 187-194; Venturi and Ferriolo, 2002). There are yet further reasons why the term "philosophy of landscape" is advisable. On the one hand, the term "landscape aesthetics" may suggest that what is at stake is a sort of history of aesthetics focused on either how landscapes were represented in art and literature or on how people aesthetically appreciated nature (Jacob 2008; Milani 2001) ([2]). On the other hand, it may suggest that the topic is a theory of what it means to aesthetically value landscapes and how people do it or even how it should be done (Bourassa 1991; Brook 2013; Carlson 2000). Finally, the term "landscape aesthetics" may sound practical in the sense that it may refer to a theory of landscape design (Gremminger 2001). What all these approaches have in common is that the fundamental question "what is a landscape?" is not raised. This is because they all make certain assumptions, even if sometimes implicit, concerning what a landscape is. The philosophy of landscape, instead, would refer to philosophical attempts at answering the above question.

If we think of its history and of the number of disciplines which refer to it, the idea of landscape turns out to be a travelling concept. A travelling concept is a concept which is coined in one discipline and subsequently imported by other disciplines so it moves across different fields (Bal 2002). As a consequence, it acquires a dynamic character in the sense that it ultimately has multiple and interdependent meanings and functions which can hardly be disentangled and thus contaminate one another. In other words, a travelling concept is heterogeneous as it is a sort of a conceptual palimpsest wherein traces of its previous itineraries are never lost but come to the surface in one way or another. Thus, it does not belong to any single field but rather bridges different disciplines. As such it is interdisciplinary and without a fixed identity.

The idea of landscape has been travelling not only through theoretical disciplines (history of art, archeology, geography, culture studies, psychology, philosophy), but also through practical fields (art, architecture, law and politics, environmental conservation, *etc.*). Its travels result in that it is "a complicated idea" which cannot be defined systematically (Thomson, Howard and Waterton 2013: 1). At the same time its travelling character cannot be dissociated from its recent career epitomized on the one hand by an attempt to define landscape studies as a separate even if transdisciplinary field and on the other by the European Landscape Convention (2000) (Antrop 2013).

The ELC is an important document for several reasons. It is the second after the UNESCO World Heritage Convention (1992) preeminent legal document which recognizes landscapes as "entities" which possess not only certain physical features, but also meanings and values and which, therefore, may and should be subject to special management. What is more, as a convention ratified by the EU member states it does have an impact on landscape policies and as such it translates into practice what theory has known for some time. However, the ELC itself has a theoretical dimension, too, as it uses a particular definition of landscape which is interesting from a philosophical standpoint due to the fact that while it suggests that the concept of landscape is to a great extent aesthetic it also offers a particular view on the aesthetic dimension of the landscape. As such it offers an insight into what can be called the "philosophy of landscape", another "field" that the concept of landscape has been travelling through. In order to see the importance of the ELC definition, it is useful to compare it with the UNESCO Convention (1992). The latter defines landscapes as follows: "Cultural landscapes are cultural properties and represent the »combined works of nature and of man«. (...) They are illustrative of the evolution of human society and settlement over time, under the influence of the physical constraints and/or opportunities presented by their natural environment and of successive social, economic and cultural forces, both external and internal." (UNESCO, 2005: 46)

The above definition draws on the previous UNESCO document (1972) which establishes general rules of protection of the cultural as well as natural heritage. The term "landscape" does not appear there and what corresponds to this concept is the idea of a cultural site defined as "a combined work of nature and of man", which is valuable from historical, ethnological, anthropological, artistic or aesthetic point of view (UNESCO, 1972, art. 1). A natural site is defined, instead, as a delineated area whose significance stems from scientific reasons as well as from its natural beauty (UNESCO, 1972, art. 2). Given that the document is in general focused on the material heritage which includes not only sites but also monuments and groups of buildings or – as far as natural heritage is concerned – natural features and geological formations, sites are seen as objects which are exceptional thanks to, among other things, their aesthetic qualities.

The 1992 Convention results from a similar attitude. However, not only does it replace the idea of site rooted in history or archeology by the concept of landscape used in geography, but also it interprets landscape in two different manners. Given that the document refers to cultural landscapes it mentions natural landscapes only indirectly. It is this indirect approach to natural landscapes that makes the document interesting from the point of view of philosophy of landscape.

In some respects the UNESCO definition treats cultural landscapes as works of art in the sense that they are human creations made of natural "stuff"[3]. To put it differently, cultural landscapes are treated here as materialized expressions of cultures. Even though their historical values are primary importance, aesthetic values are not to be excluded as they may be components of the Outstanding Universal Value described as "cultural and/or natural significance which is so exceptional as to transcend national boundaries and to be of common importance for present and future generations of all humanity" (UNESCO, 2005: 46). Seen in this light aesthetic values are trans-historical and trans-cultural, or to put it differently, objective, i.e. independent from one's point of view.

According to the 1992 document there are three sorts of cultural landscapes: clearly defined landscapes, organically evolved landscapes and associative cultural landscapes. Only in the first category are the aesthetic values explicitly included: "Clearly defined landscape [are] designed and created intentionally by man. This embraces garden and parkland landscapes constructed for aesthetic reasons (...)". (UNESCO, 2005: 120).

The aesthetic value of such landscapes is, then, inherent to them as aesthetic reasons were part of the agenda of their creators. Appreciating their beauty – UNESCO seems to equate aesthetic values with it – amounts to discovering it, i.e. to successfully reconstructing their designers' intentions and judging to what extent they have been realized. In this case the similarity between "a clearly defined landscape" and an artwork is the strongest (in fact, gardens and parks are very often treated as artworks).

The difference between this category of cultural landscape and an organically evolved landscape lies in, among other things, that the latter is not intentionally designed. Nevertheless, it may be aesthetically valuable regardless of the lack of any aesthetic purposes it is supposed to serve. As such it is very much like a natural landscape which falls under the category of the associative cultural landscape: "The inclusion of such landscapes on the World Heritage List is justifiable by virtue of the powerful religious, artistic or cultural associations of the natural element rather than material cultural evidence, which may be insignificant or even absent. (UNESCO, 2005: 121).

Given that an associative landscape falls under the general definition of cultural landscape it has to be thought of as a combined work of nature of man. However, contrary to the other two categories which result from a material interaction between nature and man, an associative landscape is, physically speaking, purely natural as the material cultural evidence may be lacking. Thus, man's work amounts to projecting onto a natural landscape his or her associations and hence an associative cultural landscape is as physical as it is conceptual. Were we to push the analogy between landscapes and artworks further, even too far, we could state that an associative landscape resembles a conceptual work of art. As far as a possible aesthetic value of such a landscape is concerned, it may be said that it stems from cultural associations and so it resides in the eye of the beholder. Even in this case, however, the aesthetic value of a landscape is seen as a property of a landscape that can be discovered through examining what sort of associations other people have with it. This is what makes associative cultural landscapes similar to designed landscapes and different from evolved landscapes.

Summing up, the UNESCO convention defines landscapes as sort of material "objects" which are to be protected because of their values, including aesthetic ones. Aesthetic values, like others, are treated as objective and are identified with exceptional beauty. It may, then, be said that gardens are beautiful because they are meant to be, evolved landscapes are "naturally" beautiful regardless of anyone's intentions or associations, whereas associative landscapes are beautiful because they are found to be beautiful by members of a culture. Obviously, this objectifying tendency results from the goals of the UNESCO and its conventions which are aimed at identifying the cultural and natural heritage in order to protect it. It means, however, that the perspective assumed in these documents is one of an expert or an outsider and not of those who simply live in the landscapes and create them intentionally or not. As a result "landscape" turns into a sort of *terminus technicus*. Moreover, it is noteworthy that landscapes are treated as "objects" which are created not only physically (designed and evolved landscapes), but also conceptually (associative landscapes).

If we agree on the above cursory interpretation of the UNESCO document, we can readily see that it corresponds to contemporary theory as well as it summarizes a long tradition. It is almost a commonplace to start every analysis of the concept of landscape with an etymological inquiry which shows that the term "landscape" used to denote either a land seen from a certain vantage point or a landscape picture (Franceschi 1992). As such it is associated with a disinterested or disengaged observation which requires distancing oneself from the world around. In other words, one may see a landscape if one assumes a theoretical attitude and is not practically involved in any interaction with his or her surroundings (Ritter 1974; Simmel 2007). Such an approach to the world is thought to be typical for post-Renaissance European culture and therefore it is possible to speak of the "invention" or "emergence" of landscape (Cauquelin 2000; Jakob 2004) as well as of its "death" (Dagognet 1982). It is, then, possible to trace its history, i.e. the history of how people perceived the world around them (Assunto 2005). The landscape-model of perception is said to be conditioned by the tradition of landscape painting which together with such categories as beauty, the sublime or the picturesque shaped aesthetic tastes, which in turn resulted in treating landscapes in purely visual terms.([4]) Another field that is said to have influenced the landscape-model of perception is literature which was a reservoir of cultural associations. To this we may add the art of gardening or landscape architecture. According to this strain of thought, landscapes are like images or, as Assunto puts it, they are nature turned into art and art turned into nature (Assunto 2005). In other words, as Roger states, landscapes are created either *in situ* when nature is made art-like (*artialisé*) by human hand as it is the case in landscape architecture or *in visu* when it is seen as if it were an artistic image created by what is seen as much as by various artistic associations (Roger 1997). This makes some scholars think that the landscape is not a universal concept and that there are cultures in which land is never perceived as a landscape (Berque 1995).

Adopting Roger's nomenclature, we can state that the UNESCO convention divides landscapes according to how they are created into *in situ* ones and *in visu* ones. However, as far as their protection is concerned the general definition treats them all as *in situ*, i.e. as sites. Referring to the emic/etic dichotomy, we can state that according to the tradition described above as well as to the UNESCO convention treating the environment in terms of landscape amounts to assuming an etic perspective, i.e. an outsider's standpoint from where landscapes appear to be "objects" which have certain values detectable only from a disengaged viewpoint from which they appear as images([5]).

The European Landscape Convention offers an emic perspective, instead. The ELC preamble states that: "(...) The landscape has an important public interest role in the cultural, ecological, environmental and social fields, (...) [it] contributes to the formation of local cultures and that it is a basic component of the European natural and cultural heritage, contributing to human well-being and consolidation of the European identity; (...) the landscape is an important part of the quality of life for people everywhere: in urban areas and in the countryside, in degraded areas as well as in areas of high quality, in areas recognized as being of outstanding beauty as well as everyday areas; (...) the landscape is a key element of individual and social well-being and that its protection, management and planning entail rights and responsibilities for everyone." (Council of Europe, 2000).

Landscapes are conceived here not as "images" viewed from a distance by a spectator, but as environments in which people are involved as active participants. In other words, the landscape is conceived more as a dwelling-place (Ingold 2000). Dwelling means being present in a place, interacting with it, giving it a sense, imbuing it with values etc. A landscape is, then, not contemplated but lived and as such it gives identity to people who inhabit it even if its own identity depends on their activities. To put it otherwise, one should not think of the landscape in terms of representation, but of actions or performances (Crouch 2013). In this sense, the ELC adopts a phenomenological perspective (Wylie 2007: 139-186) – landscapes are not so much "combined works of nature and of man" as experienced surroundings forming a sort of continua with those who experience them. As a result landscapes do not have to possess "outstanding universal values" to be protected or properly managed. On the contrary, what makes them valuable is, above all, their "everyday local value" which is crucial for one's identity and well-being. It is noteworthy that well-being used as a category decisive for landscape management (Coles and Millman, 2014) and understood as a feeling of "satisfaction of physical and biological needs and of (...) psychical and mental aspirations" (Luginbühl 2006: 32) can be thought of as an aesthetic experience. For Blanc the novelty of the ELC consists of that it provides people with a "right to aesthetics" which replaces "the right of aesthetics" (Blanc and Jollivet, 2008:205). The latter can be understood as embodied in the idea of protecting only those landscapes which have a right to be protected because of their objective, universal aesthetic values.

Despite that the above interpretation associates the idea of landscape with the concept of dwelling, it may suggest that a landscape is a "stretch of land" where people inhabit or act and thus start an ongoing interaction with it ([6]). The ELC, however, suggests much more for it defines the landscape as: "An area, as perceived by people, whose character is the result of the action and interaction of natural and/or human factors" (Council of Europe, 2000).

The above definition underlines the twofold character of landscapes. They are objective (material) and subjective (phenomenal) at the same time: they are objective in so far as they are parts of the world and subjective in so far as they are perceived by someone. It is therefore impossible to treat them simply either as "combined works of nature and man" or as images. As Le Dantec writes: "[The landscape] is not a brute fact (to say it *a la* Husserl) that can be analyzed by "calculating reason" (Heidegger) nor effect of "making art-like" (*artialisation*) (Roger) which would make it a pure invention; the landscape is (…) a mixed phenomenon in which reality and active imagination, nature and culture, geography and art overlap each other. (Le Dantec 2006: 80). Le Dantec mentions another factor that may be crucial for landscape, namely emotion. Emotion understood as *Stimmung* or atmosphere is understood less as a projection of one's emotional state onto his or her surroundings and more as a subjective-objective quality or tonality of the place that appears when someone is present there and may be felt only from within (Griffero 2014: 6-63).

It is enough to replace the term "perceive" used in the ELC definition by "experience" and to understand the latter in the broadest possible way in order to obtain a formula which fully corresponds to the above mentioned phenomenological views on landscape. The landscape cannot, then, be conceived of independently either from a subject who lives in a place and experiences it or from the place itself which is experienced by the subject. Therefore, people always are in a landscape as the term "landscape" means the lived world i.e. neither an objective reality which can be described in purely scientific terms, nor a subjective perception or experience. In other words, the term "landscape" denotes the fact the people are always in a relationship with the place they are in either permanently or only temporarily.

One of the first people to go up into mountains in order to admire a view from there was Petrarch (Ritter 1974). During his way up he is said to have met a highlander who tried to discourage him from climbing Mont Ventoux by saying that the only result the poet would obtain would be clothes torn into shreds. The highlander's attitude may be interpreted as typical for someone who is not able to appreciate the world as a landscape for he or she is lacking a proper set of cultural associations and – as a person materially engaged in it – is incapable of assuming a contemplative perspective. The peasant could not, then, see the landscape, but only the land. Such an interpretation favors the idea of landscape as a result of *artialisation*. The anecdote may be, however, interpreted in a different tone, too, namely as a story showing two different meanings of landscape. Following in the footsteps of Berleant, we could call them "observational landscape" and "landscape of engagement" (Berleant 2005). Obviously, the two landscapes are different, even if "located" in the same place, and have different aesthetic values but they are equally valid: a peasant's everyday landscape is as good as a poet's spectacular one ([7]).

What has been hitherto discussed was different definitions of landscape. The traditional definition and the phenomenological one are experience-based but only the former describes the experience involved as it states that a landscape is a land experienced as a *quasi*-artwork. In the case of the latter the question arises whether there is a particular sort of experience that can be defined as (for lack of a better word) a "landscape experience" or not.

On the one hand, if we define the landscape as the *Lebenswelt*, then we do not have to necessarily assume that there is a particular sort of experience that makes the land turn into a landscape – the land experienced in any way is landscape. On the other hand, however, there are good reasons to think that there is something like a "landscape experience" (Salwa 2014). For example, we usually do not use the term "landscape" nor do we refer to places we are in as landscapes. However, whenever we do, not only do we have in mind the land itself, but also how we experience it. When we state that this or that landscape is beautiful or interesting we refer to what we see as well as to the fact that we like it or that we find it intriguing (⁸). If asked, we can explain why we like it or find it interesting and such an explanation may reveal that we look at it as if it were a romantic picture or a kitschy photo or that we treat it as an ecological or historical curiosity. The same holds true when we say that this or that landscape is cheerful or melancholic. What is more, this sort of experience does not have to be conscious in the sense that we do not necessarily have to be capable of describing it. Sometimes we may experience sheer joy or satisfaction caused by the fact that we are physically engaged with a place as when we are walking in the woods, lying on a beach or cultivating a garden. In other words, we have a "landscape experience" when we are not focused solely on the landscape, but also on how we experience it, i.e. how it looks, smells, sounds, feels to us or how it influences us. It is true that a landscape always somehow looks, smells, sounds etc. (Porteous 1990) and that it bears an influence on us, but we usually do not notice it and only sometimes do we pay attention to it. To put it in a phenomenological vein, we may be aware not only of things but also of how they appear to us and whenever we are, we have a landscape experience.

If we, then, compare the phenomenological theory with the traditional one, it turns out that the latter describes just one sort of the landscape experience, possibly typical for someone who agrees with O. Wilde that "*Life imitates Art* far more than Art imitates Life". Yet, in order to have a landscape experience one does not have to be familiar with *The Decay of Lying*, landscape paintings or scenic photos and even with the word "landscape". When people experience their actual surroundings as a place to which they are bound and therefore they experience that they are bound to them they may be said to be having a landscape experience, too. It has to be added, though, that what is crucial is that landscapes are experienced as material and sensible, which always makes them aesthetic. This is why the idea of landscape cannot be easily replaced by the concept of environment which may eliminate any aesthetic dimension of the world as well treat it in purely objective manner (D'Angelo 2009).

Summing up, the ELC broadens the traditional definition of landscape and recognizes the role of landscapes in individual as well as social lives. At the same time, however, its aim is to enhance what can be termed as a landscape sensibility which may be said to be founded on, among other things, the landscape experience as described above. What is at stake, then, is to make people realize how important landscapes are, which can be done through making them aware of how they relate to the landscapes they live in or visit, i.e. through making them conscious of the way they perceive areas which are "combined works of nature and of man". Once this is done, people may critically reassess their relationship with their landscapes. In other words, making people sensitive to landscapes and thus able to answer the question "what is a landscape?" amounts to making them have landscape experiences.

The article was financed within the **National Programme for the Development of Humanities of the Minister of Science and Higher Education of the Republic of Poland** (2016-2019): grant nr 0059/ NPRH4/H2b/83/2016.

NOTES

[1]   See also the book *New Visions of Nature* in which one section is entitled *Philosophy of Landscape and Place* (Denthren, Keulartz and Proctor, 2009).

[2]   This approach is preceded by such books as Paulhan, 1913 or Clark, 1949.

[3]   It is a commonplace to describe landscapes as between history and nature (Assunto, 1973; D'Angelo, 2009: 26-30) or architecture and nature (Vitta, 2005).

[4]   This is why *environmental aesthetics* is critical about the idea of landscape which is accused of turning nature into art (Carlson, 2009).

[5]   Cf. Erzen, 2004

[6]   This is how e.g. J.B. Jackson explained the term "landscape" (Jackson, 1984).

[7]   Interpreted this way, the term "landscape" is similar to the term "médiance" used by A. Berque (Berque, 2000).

[8]   Other senses may be involved, too (Porteous, 1990).

BIBLIOGRAPHY

Antrop, M. (2013). A brief history of landscape research. In: P. Howard, I. H. Thompson and E. Waterton, ed., *The Routledge Companion to Landscape Studies*. New York: Routledge, pp. 12-22.

Assunto, R. (2005). *Il paesaggio e l'estetica*, 2 ed. Palermo: Novecento.

Bal, M. (2002). *Travelling concepts in the humanities: a rough guide*. Toronto: University of Toronto Press.

Berleant, A. (2005). "Down the garden path". In: A. Berleant, *Aesthetics and Environment. Variations on a Theme*, Burlington: Ashgate, pp. 31-40

Berque, A. (1995). *Les raisons du paysage*. Paris: Hazan.

Berque, A. (2000). *Médiance de milieu en paysages*. Paris: Belin.

Blanc, N., Jollivet, M. (2008). *Vers une esthétique environmentale*. Versaille: Éditions Quae.

Bourassa, S. (1991). *The Aesthetics of Landscape*. London-New York: Belhaven Press.

Brook, I. (2013). Aesthetic Appreciation of Landscapes. In: P. Howard, I. H. Thompson and E. Waterton, ed., *The Routledge Companion to Landscape Studies*. New York: Routledge, pp. 108-118

Carlson, A. (2000). *Aesthetics and the environment : the appreciation of nature, art, and architecture*. New York: Routledge.

Carlson, A. (2009). *Nature and Landscape: an Introduction to Environmental Aesthetics*. New York: Columbia University Press.

Cauquelin, A. (2000). *Invention du paysage*. Paris: PUF.

Clark, K. (1949). *Landscape into Art*. London: Murray.

Coles, R., Millman, Z. ed. (2014). *Landscape, Well-Being and Environment*. New York: Routledge.

Council of Europe (2000). *The European Landscape Convention* (available at: http://www.coe.int/en/web/conventions/full-list/-/conventions/rms/0900001680080621; accessed: 29.01.2016)

Crouch, D. (2013). Landscape, performance and performativity. In: In: P. Howard, I. H. Thompson and E. Waterton, ed., *The Routledge Companion to Landscape Studies*. New York: Routledge, pp. 119-127.

D'Angelo, P. (2009). *Filosofia del paesaggio*. Roma: Quodlibet.

Dagonet, F. (1982). *Mort du paysage?: philosophie et esthétiquedu paysage*. Seyssel: Champ Vallon.

Denthren, M., Keulartz J. and Proctor J. ed. (2009), *New Visions of Nature: Complexity and Authenticity*. Dordrecht: Springer.

Donadieu, P. (2012). *Sciences du paysage: Entre théories et pratiques*. Paris: Technique et documentations.

Erzen, J. (2004), "Ecology, art, ecological aesthetics". In: H. Strelow, ed., *Ecological Aesthetics. Art in Environmental Design: Theory and Practice*. Basel: Birkhäuser.

Franceschi, C. (1992). Du mot paysage et de ses équivalents dans cinque langues européens. In: M. Collot, ed., *Les enjeux du paysage*. Bruxelles: Ousia.

Gremminger, Th. (2001). *Esthétique du paysage; guide pour la planification et la conception de projets*. Berne : Office fédéral de l'environnement, des forêts et du paysage.

Griffero, T. (2014). Atmospheres: Aesthetics of Emotional Spaces. Farnham: Ashgate.

Howard, P., Thompson, I.H. and Waterton E., ed. (2013). *The Routledge Companion to Landscape Studies*. New York: Routledge.

Ingold, T. (2000). *The perception of the environment: essays on livelihood, dwelling & skill*. New York: Routledge.

Jackson, J. B. (1984) *Discovering the vernacular landscape*. New Haven: Yale University Press.

Jakob, M. (2004). *L'émergence du paysage*. Gollion: Infolio.

Jakob, M. (2008). *Le paysage*. Gollion: Infolio.

Le Dantec, J.-P. (2006), Philosophie du paysage. In: A. Berque ,ed., *Mouvance II*. Paris: Éditions de la Villette, pp. 80-83.

Luginbühl, Y. (2006), Bien-être et paysage. In: A. Berque ,ed., *Mouvance II*. Paris: Éditions de la Villette, pp. 32-33.

Milani, R. (2001). *L'arte del paesaggio*. Bologna: Il mulino.

Paulhan, F. (1913). *L'ésthetique du paysage*. Paris: Alcan.

Porteous, D. (1990). *Landscapes of the mind : worlds of sense and metaphor*. Toronto: Toronto University Press.

Ritter, J. (1974). Landschaft. Zur Funktion des Ästhetischen in der modernen Gesellschaft. In: J. Ritter, *Subjektivität*. Frankfurt/M.: Suhrkamp, pp. 141-163, 172-190

Roger, A. (1997). *Court traité du paysage*. Paris: Gallimard.

Salwa, M. (2014). Krajobraz jako doświadczenie estetyczne. In: B. Frydryczak, M. Ciesielski, ed., *Krajobraz kulturowy*, Poznan: PTPN, pp. 43-52.

Simmel, G. (2007). The Philosophy of Landsape. *Theory, Culture & Society*, 24(7-8), pp. 20-29.

UNESCO (1972). *Convention Concerning the Protection of the World Cultural and Natural Heritage* (available at: http://whc.unesco.org/en/conventiontext/ [accessed: 29.01.2016]

UNESCO (2005). *Basic Texts of the 1972 World Heritage Convention*. Paris: UNESCO.

Venturi Ferriolo, M. (2002), *Etiche del paesaggio: il progetto del mondo umano*. Roma: Editori uniti.

Verríssimo Serrão, A. (2013). *Filosofia da Paisagem. Estudos*. Lisboa: Centro de Filosofia da Universidade de Lisboa.

Vitta, M. (2005). *Il paesaggio: una storia fra natura e architettura*. Torino: Einaudi

Wylie, J. (2007). *Landscape*. New York: Routledge.

THE RELATIONSHIP BETWEEN HUMAN COMMUNITIES AND LANDSCAPE OF THE NEOLITHIC PERIOD – PHENOMENOLOGY IN LANDSCAPE

Renata Zych
Pracownia Archeologiczna "Krzemień", Rzeszów

ABSTRACT

Basic category which can be used by an archaeologist is landscape. Considering phenomenology, the landscape is treated as a sphere of human activity, creation, influence. A phenomenological method allows us to understand the "living world". An archaeologist is trying to get to the meanings of the social world that used to be for human being in the prehistory and notice what cultural patterns used to guide their actions.
The aim of this study is to examine the meaning of landscape regarding the Neolithic cemeteries of the Funnel Beaker culture. So it is a matter concerning the sphere of "sacrum" aspect of the symbolism derived from sepulchral rituals. The range of sources includes cemeteries of megalithic graves, so-called Kujavian long barrows. The great structures of the Kujavian barrows indicate a strong emphasis which was put on their visibility and materiality, and thus on the mutual interaction, modification and shaping of the landscape, but their construction meant not only the physical but also a mental change in the landscape. Owing to their durability they also had impact on future communities.

Keywords
Landscape, Neolithic, Kujavian barrows, phenomeology

1. INTRODUCTION

Basic category which can be used by an archaeologist is landscape. Considering phenomenology, the landscape is treated as a sphere of human activity, creation, influence. In archaeology, it is important to reach the prehistoric perception and symbolism of landscape (Tilley 1993).

Phenomenological perspective is not uniform. As for archaeology, it uses both, philosophy of Martin Heidegger (Karlsson 2000) as well as Hannah Arendt (Staaf 2000). Additionally, there are also common references to Mircea Eliade in both older and younger literature (e.g. Makiewicz, Prinke 1980; Posern-Zieliński 1983; Kowalewska-Marszałek 2000; Woźny 2000). This approach has become particularly preferred by modern humanistic geography. Now indications leading to the understanding of the people in their environment are being searched. There are two basic approaches to the problem of landscape in a phenomenological trend. The first one, starting with the measurement of physical space and its description, designed to grasp a process in which the environment becomes a part of human activity and experience. The second one is coming from a description of its experience, organization, creation, in other words, how people "humanize" distinguished from each other, designate, and inhabit different parts of space. However, the common denominator is the assumption, that "places are not neutral and objective segments of physical space, but the area of the specific human involvement" (Reverse 1996: 50). Phenomenological reflection is a denial of the abstract treatment of a man, the world and is a constructive proposal to rebuild the relationship between a subject and object. Considering the innumerable spatial facts it is possible to find the world of relations and places saturated with different meanings. A phenomenological method allows us to understand the "living world". An archaeologist is trying to get to the meanings of the social world that used to be for human being in the prehistory and notice what cultural patterns used to guide their actions. The actions are intentional and serve a specific purpose, they have certain meaning, but the discovery of their significance requires knowledge of the motives and methods of the participant's conceptualization of the space in that cultural reality. The method of studying the point begins with facts and things, and leads to know the over-individual experiences - "patterns of culture" or, in other words, mental premises, the general orientations which by means of conceptualization stage, contributed their content to the sepulchral spaces, shaping them in a certain way. Eschatological value of cemeteries especially justifies this non-semantic level of meaning (Eliade 1993: 53-55).

Speaking of archaeology, the studies of the landscape were most commonly associated with the so-called settlement archaeology and considerations took into account those aspects of human life which were associated with the sphere of "profanum" thus, dwellings, settlements and the relationship between settlements or social structures. The aim of this study is to examine the symbolism of landscape regarding the Neolithic cemeteries of the Funnel Beaker culture. So it is a matter concerning the sphere of "sacrum" aspect of the symbolism derived from sepulchral rituals. The range of sources includes cemeteries of megalithic graves, so-called Kujavian long barrows.

2. THE CONSTRUCTION OF KUJAVIAN BARROWS

In Poland, as mentioned above, one of the types of megalithic graves are so-called "Kujavian barrows". Their origin is connected with the Funnel Beaker culture (TRB) people (Wiślański 1979: 256). Kujavian barrows are located in three clusters: 1 – in the territory of Western Pomerania, 2 - Central Pomerania, 3 – in the area of Kujavia and Chelmno Land (Fig. 1).

The Kujavian barrows found in Central Pomerania are classified as the same type of megalithic tombs as the Kujavian barrows from the two other regions mentioned above, although they differ from them to some degree.

The TRB culture would construct Kujavian barrows in the Kujavia region, Chełmno Land and Western Pomerania on a plan resembling a triangle. The construction of the barrows was to a large extent homogenous, while the differences concerned mainly their size. The length of the tombs varies from 6 m in Łabuń Wielki to 170 m in Rzeszynek. The width of the barrows at the apex is generally impossible to determine because of the substantial destruction of this part. Where such measurements could be taken, it varied from 2 m in Kłęby to 3.5 m also on this site. In most cases barrows were oriented east-west with their base located in the east, sometimes with some deviations towards the north and south. Barrows oriented differently were built rarely. The mound of Kujavian barrows was made from earth; among the exceptions are the barrows with an earth-and-stone mound from Krępcewo and Janiszewko and stone triangles from Piotrkowo, Lubraniec and Sampolno (Zych 2002: 50). These mounds were surrounded by massive stone slabs which, initially larger at the front (higher) part of the structure, were subsequently decreasing in size towards the top (lower) part of the mound (Jażdżewski 1970: 16). Apart from the large stones, the earthwork was also surrounded by small pebbles which supported the construction (Wiślański 1977: 85). The large blocks were specially selected so as to achieve the effect of a smooth external wall (Chmielewski 1952: 17). The barrows contain inhumation burials. The bodies were laid in the upright position, along the long axis of the barrow, rarely crosswise, mostly in the front part of the barrow. The dead were buried in cavities below the original surface or on the surface, sometimes surrounded by stone slabs or covered with slabs or on a stone slab. Sometimes several combinations were applied at once and on other occasions burials were left without any shielding. The dead were usually buried individually (Zych 2002: 52). Among the exceptions are the burials in Wietrzychowice and Sarnowo. In Wietrzychowice,

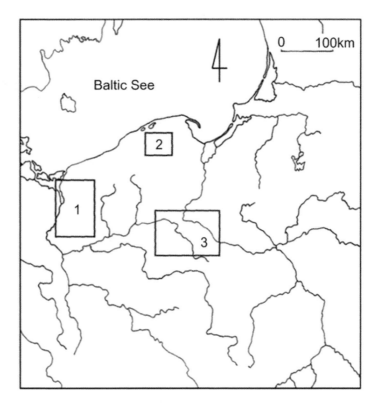

Fig.1. Localisation of Kujavian barrows. 1 – Western Pomerania, 2 – Central Pomerania, 3 – Kujavia-Chelmno Land.

in barrow no. 5 the discovered burial contained two skeletons, probably of a female and male (Makiewicz 1969: 27), although Kapica identified both as males (Kapica 1970: 148, 150; Jadczykowa 1971: 135). While in Sarnowo in barrow no. 2, in grave no. 1 a pit with two skeletons was discovered whose sex has not been identified. In many barrows the traces of burial pits were discovered with no skeletons preserved (Chmielewski 1952: 17). Structures related to cult were also discovered in the Kujavian barrows, made both of wood and stone, as well as the so-called fire-middens, probably the remains of the funeral feast (Zych 2002: 53) (Fig. 2).

The construction of megalithic barrows in Central Pomerania includes some extraordinary traits. What now are compact cemeteries, in the past could consist of 30 barrows. Among the characteristic components of their design are: a large number of barrows cramped in a small area and a large variation in their orientation in comparison to the almost unified orientation of the Kujavian barrows found in the previously presented areas (Jankowska 1980: 97). The length of these barrows varies from 12 m on site no. 2 in Łupawa to 90 m on site no. 15 in Łupawa. The width of barrows at the base varies from 3 m on site no. 15 and 2a in Łupawa to 10 m on site no. 18 in Łupawa, the width at the top varies from 2 m on site no. 2a in Łupawa to 5 m on the same site. The barrows were usually oriented north-south with minor deviations from the norm. Some of them had different orientation. The barrows were constructed on the plan of an elongated trapezoid. Also rectangular barrows could be found. The mounds of barrows in Central Pomerania were stone-earthen and surrounded by large stone slabs. Analogically to the constructions presented above, the largest blocks formed the front wall of funeral structures and their size was decreasing gradually toward the top. They were carefully selected and positioned so that the smooth wall faced outward. The height of the stones was regulated by the depth at which they were placed in the ground. Great blocks were supported from both sides by small pebbles which would often form a wide bench on the external side, which secured the stone structure from sliding down (Zych 2002: 54). Both inhumation burials as well as cremation burials were identified in the barrows. The burials were probably situated in the front and top parts of the barrow (Weber 1983: 61). Since the skeletons in most cases did not survive, the place of burial must be determined by the archaeological analysis of the scattering of the mobile source material. The dead were buried in pit graves surrounded by stones or covered with stone slabs or placed in flat graves directly under the mound. In most cases the burial was intended for one person. Also traces of cult hearths were identified (Zych 2002: 55) (Fig. 3). The characteristic feature of the Kuyavian barrows from Central Pomerania is the presence of *stellas,* centre stones, which according to Kośko (1972: 227) are a component common to dolmen architecture not occurring in the Kujavian barrows from other areas.

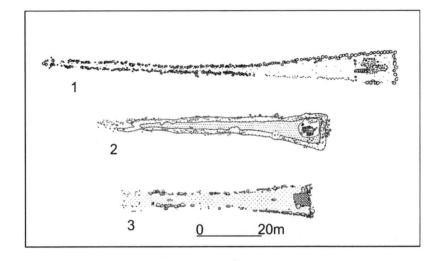

Fig.2. Kujavia and Chelmno Land. Plan of Kujavian barrows: 1 – Wietrzychowice site 1; 2 – Sarnowo site 1; Gaj site 1 (after: Rzepecki 2011: 80 fig. 65 – changed).

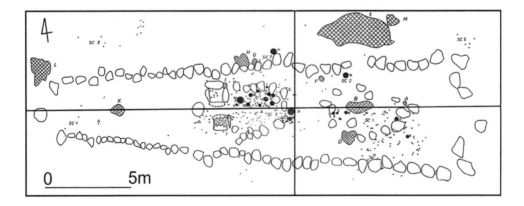

Fig.3. Central Pomerania. Plan of Kujavia barrow 5. Łupawa site 2 (after Wierzbicki 1992: 34 fig. 24 – changed).

3. KUJAVIAN BARROWS IN THE LANDSCAPE

As was mentioned above, one of the approaches of phenomenology refers to the perception and the experience of physical landscape by the description and observation of the natural environment which becomes part of the human activity. Therefore, the location of the cemeteries was not accidental. It depended on the topography of the place, type of soil and other features of the landscape. The Kujavian barrows from the areas of Western Pomerania, Kujavia region and Chełmno Land are usually situated on a flat or slightly hilly territory, sometimes on a small hill, not far from water reservoirs or wetlands, which is partly related to the nature of the geographical area. Site no. 4 in Krępcewo represents this type of area. It is situated in a high point of a postglacial high plain, which extends between the valley of the Ina river and the valley of the Mała Ina river. Its surface is quite varied, crossed by watercourses and numerous small lakes and wetlands. The barrow was formed on the highest elevation of postglacial high plain on a naturally extended, poorly visible land hump (Wiślański 1977: 83).

In the area of Central Pomerania, Kujavian barrows were situated on the right bank of the Łupawa river, typically on the first terrace and within the distance of 200 m to 800 m from the river. Barrows located outside the first terrace were situated farther from the river within the distance exceeding 20 km (Jankowska 1980: 79-82). Individual megalithic structures were mostly situated on level ground. Rarely were they built on small hills (Wierzbicki 1992: 76).

The presented relation, although visible between the barrows and components of the physical landscape, does not amount to environmental determinism. The capabilities and constraints of the natural environment and its resources had an impact on cultural behaviour to a certain extent. However, a more important role was attributed to the fact how these physical, objectively existing landscape features were perceived by the communities which constructed these megaliths: what meaning they were given and what image was presented in the minds of the constructors. Together with the appearance of the impressive structures of the Kujavian barrows, the current physical landscape also underwent a transformation. Raw materials such as wood, earth, and stones were gathered in great quantities and later used for the construction of megalithic structures. The use of such huge amounts of raw materials had an impact on the physical transformation of the areas which provided these raw materials. As Goldhahn aptly put it, at the same time a monument is materialised in the landscape, the landscape is materialised in a monument (2008: 59). The construction of barrows did not bring only physical changes to the landscape. The social and ritual execution of megalithic structures used to incorporate raw materials by transforming them in a new construction which obtained its own importance as a whole. The change also concerned the entire landscape. Together with a new barrow appeared a new category which, with its significance as a whole, affected the meaning of the surroundings. Megalithic structures were not only perceived through their relationship with the physical landscape (natural environment). Their image was being created and shaped also in relation to the cultural landscape. Among the important factors were: the location of settlements, places of worship, nature of the economy, land arrangement left by the previous communities, etc. A clear example of this phenomenon seems to be reflected in the site in Flintbek where graves appear to be related to settlements and the arrangement of fields, which can be suggested by sediment cavities found nearby or even beneath larger graves and by the traces of ploughing (Mischka 2011: 757). In the case of the Kuyavian barrows from Western Pomerania, Kujavia or Chełmno Land, the fact that there had been no research conducted into the settlements makes the carrying out of an analysis of spatial relation between particular Kujavian barrows with their contemporary settlements impossible. However, it has been observed that megaliths of this group were located where previous TRB settlements had been set up. This situation occurred in Sarnowo where the traces of ploughing were found beneath barrow no. 8 (Chmielewski 1952: 34-39), whereas remnants of settlement sediments were found beneath barrow no. 9 (Wiklak 1986: 16). In Zberzyn also beneath the mound of the barrow the remains of fertile brown earths were found which may suggest that the area had originally been used for farming (Gorczyca 1981: 15). In the area of the micro-region of Łupawa (Central Pomerania) two settlement groups were located: western and eastern. The western group consisted of a permanent, multi-phase settlement together with the campsites located within a small distance, cemetery and single megalithic barrows. The eastern group was of a similar nature. Also here a permanent settlement (non-localised) constituted a central point surrounded by cemeteries or sites of other nature (Jankowska 1980: 77; Weber 1983: 3). In the presented model both groups form the same settlement arrangement where the main role is played by the permanent settlement. A different model of settlement structure for this region was developed by Wierzbicki. He identified one system which contained all important settlement features. The settlement was a central point whereas the Kujavian barrows determined zones which were explored by the community (1999: 202). A common feature of both models is the central position of the permanent settlement. In both cases the location of barrows, although they played an important role, was determined by the location of the settlement. This confirms the evolution of megalith importance also in relation to the cultural aspects of the landscape. Both the physical and cultural landscapes form a structured whole. The second approach in phenomenology puts more emphasis on these aspects of cultural landscape and therefore ways to organize, designate, and humanise the inhabited area. It was the significance that the barrow had for a given community that played the most important role.

In archaeology, the basic concept of burial is the grave. According to the simplest approach, the grave is the place where the deceased is buried. The tomb is a more elaborate version of the grave (Wierzbicki 2006: 88). The concept of the grave leads to another one, which is burial. The word "burial" can be understood differently. If it refers to a given individual – e.g. "the burial of a man" – it indicates a specific deceased lodged in a certain place and, in fact, it corresponds to the concept of the grave. Burial is also understood in a more extensive way. It refers to the whole script of actions whose purpose is to place the deceased in the grave. These actions may take a more or less extensive and complex form. The tomb is therefore intended for the deceased but the death of a member of the community entails various actions, the effects of which relate to the religious, social and economic sphere. Death as well as practices related to constructing the tomb and rituals that accompanied them absorbed members of the community and therefore affected every aspect of an individual's and the whole community's lives. The great structures of the Kujavian barrows indicate a strong emphasis which was put on their visibility and materiality, and thus on the mutual interaction, modification and shaping of the landscape. The basic concept behind megalithic constructions was their permanence. Their construction meant not only the physical but also a mental change in the landscape. Owing to their durability they also had impact on future communities. The communities of the Neolithic Globular Amphora Culture sometimes incorporated graves of their dead into the mounds of the Kujavian barrows (Tetzlaff 1961: 43). Also burial kurgans of the Corded Ware culture of the late Neolithic period as well as the burial kurgans of the Lusatian Culture of the Bronze Age were found in the vicinity of these megaliths (Wierzbicki 1992: 80). Probably their importance for subsequent communities was different. But this is the evidence of their significant impact on the environment and how it is perceived not only by the community contemporary to the barrows but also future communities to the present day.

4. CONCLUSIONS

The Kujavian barrows shaped both the physical and the cultural landscape. They constituted a central point in the landscape for subsequent graves. The future location of barrows was determined by the past and current location of barrows. People not only remembered places where the barrows had been raised in the past, but also recognized unoccupied places in the landscape as places where future generations would construct their barrows. Such practices are ingrained in such factors as: local natural conditions, agricultural practices and cultural tradition. The barrow could survive individuals and generations absorbing the memories of the previous inhabitants. If the structure of tombs survived throughout further periods, it meant something more than only a funeral ritual. The megalith also became a lasting artefact which testified to the previous inhabitants of the land. In the past the construction of funeral structures was tantamount to leaving a lasting mark in the landscape. Owing to this, the past could be absorbed by present generations and re-interpreted by future ones. There is no doubt that the construction of the Kujavian barrows took place in a highly ritualised and organised landscape.

BIBLIOGRAPHY

Chmielewski, W. (1952). *Zagadnienia grobowców kujawskich w świetle ostatnich badań*. Łódź: Wydawnictwo Muzeum Archeologicznego w Łodzi.

Eliade, M. (1993). *Sacrum, mit, historia*. Warszawa: Państwowy Instytut Wydawniczy.

Goldhahn J. (2008). From Monuments in Landscape to Landscapes in Monuments: Monuments, Death and Landscape in Early Bronze Age Scandinavia. In: A. Jones, ed., *Prehistoric Europe. Theory and practice*, 1-st ed. Chichester: Wiley-Blackwell, pp. 56-85.

Gorczyca, K. (1981). Grobowiec kujawski w Zberzynie, woj. Konin. *Fontes Archaeologici Posnanienses*, 30, pp. 1-19.

Jadczykowa, I. (1971). Sprawozdanie z końcowego etapu prac badawczych na neolitycznym cmentarzysku grobowców kujawskich w Wietrzychowicach, pow. Koło. *Prace i Materiały Muzeum archeologicznego i Etnograficznego w Łodzi*, 18, pp. 93-103.

Jankowska, D. (1980). *Kultura pucharów lejkowatych na Pomorzu Środkowym. Grupa Łupawska*. Poznań: Uniwersytet Adama Mickiewicza.

Jażdżewski, K. (1970). Związki grobowców kujawskich w Polsce z grobami megalitycznymi w Niemczech Północnych, w Danii i w krajach zachodnioeuropejskich. *Prace i Materiały Muzeum Archeologicznego i Etnograficznego w Łodzi*, 17, pp. 15-36.

Kapica, Z. (1970). Pochówki neolityczne z grobowców kujawskich w Wietrzychowicach, pow. Koło, w świetle badań antropologicznych. *Prace i Materiały Muzeum Archeologicznego i Etnograficznego w Łodzi*, 17, pp. 145-155.

Karlsson, H. (2000). Why Is There Material Culture Rather than Nothing? Heideggerian thoughts and archaeology. In: C. Holtorf and C, H. Karlsson ed., *Phisolophy and Archaeological Practice. Perspectives for the 21st Century*, 1-st ed. Göteborg: Bricoleur Press, pp. 69-86.

Kośko, A. (1972). Badania na cmentarzysku "megalityczym" w Łupawie (stanowisko 15) w powiecie słupskim. *Koszalińskie Zeszyty Muzealne*, 2, pp. 224-236.

Kowalewska-Marszałek, H. (2000). Kontynuacja osadnicza, a zmiana kulturowa – na przykładzie badań cmentarzyska w Kicharach Nowych koło Sandomierza. In: S. Tabaczyński ed., *Kultury archeologiczne a rzeczywistość dziejowa*, 1-st ed., Warszawa: Wydawnictwo Naukowe PWN, pp. 69-74.

Makiewicz, T. (1969). Cmentarzysko grobowców kujawskich w Wietrzychowicach, pow. Koło. *Sprawozdania Archeologiczne*, 21, pp. 25-28.

Makiewicz, T. and Prinke, A. (1980). Teoretyczne możliwości identyfikacji miejsc sakralnych. *Przegląd Archeologiczny*, 28, pp. 57-90.

Mischka, D. (2011). The Neolithic burial sequence at Flintbek LA3, north Germany, and its cart tracks: a precise chronology. *Antiquity* 85(329), pp. 742-758.

Posern-Zieliński, A. (1983). Inspiracja fenomenologiczna w archeologicznych studiach nad religiami społeczeństw pradziejowych. Refleksje religioznawcze. *Przegląd Archeologiczny*, 30, pp. 187-200.

Rewers, E. (1996). *Język i przestrzeń w poststrukturalistycznej filozofii kultury*. Poznań: Uniwersytet Adama Mickiewicza.

Rzepecki, S. (2011). *U źródeł megalityzmu w kulturze pucharów lejkowatych*. Łódź: Instytut Archeologii Uniwersytetu Łódzkiego, Fundacja Uniwersytetu Łódzkiego.

Staff, B. M. (2000). Hannah Arendt and Torsten Hägerstrand. Converging tendencies in contemporary archaeological theory?. In: C. Holtorf and C, H. Karlsson ed., *Phisolophy and Archaeological Practice. Perspectives for the 21st Century,* 1-st ed. Göteborg: Bricoleur Press, pp. 135-152.

Tetzlaff, W. (1961). Grobowce kultury pucharów lejkowatych ze Zberzynka, pow. Konin i Obałek, pow. Koło, *Fontes Archaeologici Posnanienses,* 12, pp. 40-51.

Tilley, C. (1993). *A Phenomenology of Landscape. Places, Paths and Monument.* Oxford: Berg.

Weber, A. (1983). *Studia nad obrządkiem pogrzebowym grupy łupawskiej KPL.* Poznań: Uniwersytet Adama Mickiewicza.

Wierzbicki, J. (1992). *Cmentarzysko kultury pucharów lejkowatych w Łupawie, woj. Słupsk, stanowisko 2.* Poznań: Uniwersytet Adama Mickiewicza.

Wierzbicki, J. (1999). *Łupawski mikroregion osadniczy ludności kultury pucharów lejkowatych.* Poznań: Uniwersytet Adama Mickiewicza.

Wierzbicki, J. (2006). Megality kultury pucharów lejkowatych – czy tylko grobowce?. In: J. Libera and K. Tunia, eds., *Idea megalityczna w obrządku pogrzebowym kultury pucharów lejkowatych,* 1-st ed. Lublin-Kraków: Instytut Archeologii PAN, Oddział w Krakowie, Instytut Archeologii UMCS w Lublinie, pp. 87-102.

Wiklak, H. (1986). Podsumowanie wyników badań wykopaliskowych w obrębie grobowca 9 w Sarnowie, województwo włocławskie. *Prace i Materiały Muzeum Archeologicznego i Etnograficznego w Łodzi,* 33, pp. 5-21.

Wiślański, T. (1977). Bezkomorowy grobowiec megalityczny (tzw. kujawski) w Krępcewie nad Iną, stan. 4, gm. Kolin, woj. Szczeci. *Sprawozdania Archeologiczne,* 29, pp. 83-100.

Wislański, T. (1979). Kształtowanie się miejscowych kultur rolniczo-hodowlanych. Plemiona kultury pucharów lejkowatych. In: W. Hensel and T. Wiślański, ed., *Prahistoria Ziem Polskich. Neolit,* 2, 1 st ed. Wrocław-Warszawa-Kraków-Gdańsk: Ossolineum, pp. 165-261.

Woźny, J. (2000). *Symbolika przestrzeni miejsc grzebalnych w czasach ciałopalenia zwłok na ziemiach polskich.* Bydgoszcz: Wyższa Szkoła Pedagogiczna.

Zych, R. (2002). *Wielkie domostwa i grobowce typu kujawskiego w kulturze symbolicznej neolitu na ziemiach polskich.* Rzeszów: Instytut Archeologii UR, Rzeszowski Oddział SNAP.

CULTURAL HUMANISTIC GEOGRAPHY.
CONTRIBUTIONS TO THE DISCUSSION OF LANDSCAPE
AS HERITAGE

Luciene Cristina Risso
UNESP (São Paulo State University), Brazil

ABSTRACT

The landscape concept emerged in the context of Geography, during Century XIX. Nowadays taken by various fields of knowledge, the landscape takes on the multiple senses. However, the way I want to track in this article, in order to contribute to the heritage discussion, refers to current contributions of Cultural Geography, mainly the Cultural Humanist Geography, to which has the proposal to understand and appreciate the subjectivity. That is, the experiences, the meanings, the tangible and intangible values associated with landscapes. The symbol of this theoretical current linked to the publication of Tuan, in 1976, of the article entitled Humanist Geography. The adopted methodology is the literature review, focusing the trajectory of the landscape concept in Geography. This geographic chain can contribute to the theoretical and methodological debate of the landscape as heritage, towards enhancement of landscapes by the experiences and individual and collective memories, as well as the landscape of practice, with the participation of the people in their management process.

Keywords
Perception, Landscape, Cultural humanistic geography, theory, heritage

1. INTRODUCTION

The landscape word, during the XVI century, was related to the art, but as a scientific term, the word landscape (Landschaft) was introduced in the XIX century by Humboldt (1769-1859), the great naturalist. He defined it as "the character of the Earth region" (Naveh and Lieberman 1984: 4).

Friedrich Ratzel (1844-1904) introduced the culture as a key factor of human geography and for the first time, appeared the term cultural geography (Culturgeographie). Another important geographer, in the culture – landscape discussion, was Otto Schlüter (1872-1959). Otto said that "the brand men imposes on the landscape is the fundamental object of all research" (Shlüter 1952-1954, 1958 apud Claval 2001: 24).

Ratzel and Shlüter point to the limitations of the culture concept, precisely because of the Darwinian influence that assigns, exclusively, to the tools and techniques the domination of the medium, leaving aside "(...) the attitudes and beliefs" of people (Claval 2001: 27, apud Risso 2008: 69).

The research of the Siegfried Passarge (1866-1958) was also relevant for the landscape' study. In 1913, he used the term "landscape geography" (Landschaftskunde), explaining that the landscape is "the set of what the eye can encompass" (Claval 2001:29). Their comparative analyzes of landscapes serve as a model in Germany and abroad. The landscape study focused on cultural events dominated the German geography from the 1920's until 1960 (Claval 2001: 29).

In addition, it should be the Germans differentiated conception of natural landscape (naturlandschaften) and cultural landscape (kulturlandschaften). Indeed, it was Carl Sauer (1889-1975), German geographer, who introduced the notion of natural landscape and cultural landscape of American Geography (Risso 2008: 69). Sauer was the precursor to the rescue of landscape studies, by founding the school of Berkeley, in 1922. Her thoughts were broadcast around the world, encouraging the creation of many "cultural geography" courses (Holzer 2008: 137).

For Sauer (1889-1975) in "The Morphology of Landscape", published in 1925, "the culture is the agent, the natural area is the medium, the cultural landscape is the result" (Sauer 1998: 343) (1), it is the same as one supra organic entity (influence of Kroeber), above society that builds. Sauer has become an exponent of cultural studies, founding what might be called the American Cultural Geography.

Grounded in the conceptions, the Sauer' disciples: Wagner and Mikesell, in 1962, said the landscape is "a heritage of a long natural evolution and of many generations of human efforts" (Wagner; Mikesell 2003: 35-36).

However, around the 1950s and 1960s, cultural studies come into decay, facing a new reality of the world, emerging, in this context, new scientific theoretical and methodological matrices. Within the Geography, arises the New Geography (or theoretical-neopositivist geography), based on mathematical and physical principles; the Humanist Geography (identified later by Tuan as Cultural Humanist Geography, see Holzer 2008: 146) and the New Cultural Geography, based on Marxist assumptions.

1.1. Remarks / Methodology

The adopted methodology is the literature review, focusing the trajectory of the landscape concept in Geography.

2. CURRENT CULTURAL GEOGRAPHY: TRAJECTORIES AND LANDSCAPE DEFINITIONS OF CULTURAL HUMANIST GEOGRAPHY AND THE NEW CULTURAL GEOGRAPHY

The humanist cultural geography is an approach that followed a philosophical aspect contrary to the precepts of other positivist perspectives, such as Traditional Geography and the New Geography (neopositivist). Their philosophical base comprises the authors of phenomenology, especially from Husserl (1913) (2), Heidegger (1927) (3), Merleau-Ponty (1945) (4) and Bachelard (1957) (5).

At the beginning of the XXI century, other philosophical bases have been used in geography, considered as poststructuralist (Deleuze), and post-phenomenology, with Ricoeur (2004), Derrida (1994), Idhe (1993), Nancy (1991) among others. These authors glimpse "think phenomenology in the current context, i.e. make the phenomenology a philosophy of the XXI century" (Marandola Jr. 2013: 57).

From the perspective of Tuan (1976), "make philosophy may be the human activity par excellence, for its basic characteristic is the reflection" (Tuan 1982:145) (6). For him, the humanist Geography studies the geographical knowledge, or rather, as individuals and social groups acquires knowledge and spatial skills, with their range of experiences.

Tuan notes that the competence of a humanist linked to the interpretation of human experience in its ambiguity, ambivalence and complexity. Its main function as a geographer is to clarify the meaning of concepts, symbols and aspirations, as they relate to space and place. Several authors of the Geography accept this approach, and in this article, let us highlight a few, trying to orient so summarized its proposals for the Geography.

The work of Dardel (1952), which went "unnoticed in France" (Claval 2001:53), was rediscovered in North America (Canada). It consists of a geographical reflection, which considers the human relationship with the earth is more profound than you think. It is more than material, it is telluric, one geographicity that enables man to understand his existence.

Contextualized in this proposal, the goal is to find the primitive or telluric experience, i.e. the space of feelings and imagination with Earth in its geographical areas and landscapes.

Dardel (2011: 97) does not dismisses the science, but suggests that Geography should not give "unreservedly to the science" because understanding the world is also "moral, aesthetic and spiritual".

In his view, the landscape is "une convergence, un moment vécu. Un lien interne, une 'impression', unit tous les elements". He adds: "une échappee vers toute la Terre, une fenêtre sur des possibilites illimittées: un horizon. Non une ligne fixe, mais un mouvement, un élan" (Dardel 1952: 41-42). Signifying that the landscape has its own dynamicity and what it will become in the future understand, always, a universe of possibilities, because of human capacity for creation (Risso 2008:73).

Lowenthal, in 1961, proposes a geographical epistemology based on experience and imagination. Based on what Wright called geosophy (geosophy), ie "the nature and expression of geographical ideas, both past and present" and "all manner of people" (Wright 1947:12 apud Lowenthal, 1982:104) (7) as well as his conception of Terrae Incognitae, Lowenthal explains his essay on the theory of geographical knowledge, as he defines himself as well.

According to Wright (1947), the whole earth is a vast miscellany of Terrae Incognitae miniature, ie "the parts of the private worlds not incorporated in the overall picture". As people will acquire new experiences with new places, this becomes terrae cognita, which goes beyond knowledge, it is "much more localized and restricted in space and time" (Wright 1947 apud Lowenthal 1982: 118).

The thought of Lowenthal emphasizes environmental perception study (or world) of people from different cultures, because although we share common perceptions, "the Earth's surface is drawn up for each person by refraction through cultural and personal lenses, habits and fantasies" (Lowenthal 1982: 41). Thus, the ideas and images have a time dimension and are shared by different cultures.

The epistemological research of the author relates, among other things, on "how the geography of the horizon varies between individuals and groups" (Lowenthal 1982: 104). This is the wealth of this geography, always envisioning interpret new places, new cultures, transforming terrae incognitae in terrae cognita.

Tuan (1961), inspired by the poetic work of Bachelard (1957), uses the term experience as the key to understanding human relationships with their spaces and places. To experience, according to Tuan (1983:10) "is to learn; it means acting on the data and create from it". For him, the experience involves a web of feelings, perceptions and ideas, emotions and thoughts. Therefore, "the human spaces reflect the quality of your senses and your mind" (Tuan 1983:18).

Tuan and Lowenthal, years later (1965) held a meeting in which they gave "a new direction to the process of renewal of Geography" (Holzer 2008: 138).

In 1976, after the creation of a geographic basis grounded in Existentialist Phenomenology, was the manifest of "Humanist Geography" with Humanistic Geography (Tuan 1976).

According to Holzer (2008: 141), of the phenomenological method was appropriate, especially the concepts of "lived world" and "being in the world", that geography would be identified with the concept of "place". There has not been, however, a strict enforcement of concern of the phenomenological method proposed by Husserl.

Anne Buttimer, in 1976, used the existential phenomenology and, through the concept of world, it says this is a "dynamic unity and is experienced holistically, until the thought start to think about it" (Buttimer 1982:171) (8). The authoress aims at a dialogue between phenomenology and Geography, a humanistic orientation with the experiential base.

To Buttimer (1982: 166) "the humanistic geographer attuned to the voices of the scientist and philosopher, can not give up the luxury of ignoring anything that might shed light on the complexities of man's relationship with the Earth". It uses concepts such as intersubjectivity and world/space lived. However, intersubjectivity is fundamental because "taken both to cultural heritage as in social interaction, could help unite the social and collective dimensions of human experience" (Buttimer 1982: 192).

Another important author is Edward Relph (1976), which cites the work of Dardel (1952) and "contributed a lot with reflections on place, landscape and geographic ontology, especially from Heidegger" (Marandola JR 2013: 52). Relph shows that personal experiences, present in places, are steeped in meaning and values. The assignment of values entered by us in the landscapes, demonstrates how much we are involved emotionally with them.

Collot (1990: 22), in turn, has asserted that mutual dependence between perceived landscape and the subject has a double meaning: "while the horizon, the landscape merges with the visual field of the person who observes, but in return all consciousness and awareness of ... the subject merges with the horizon and is defined as being in the world".

The humanist geography, now identified as Humanist Cultural Geography, created "an eclecticism proposals and extrapolating the initial public cultural and historical American Geographers" (Holzer 2008: 143).

Nonetheless, in the late 1980s, there was a decline in the research of the Humanist Cultural Geography, since according Marandola Jr. (2013: 52), was "a time of prevalence of Marxist discussions."

In parallel with these discussions of humanistic cultural geography, several cultural geographers followed other analytical methods.

It can be considered that there was, in the 1970s, a rupture with the classic and traditional thinking in cultural geography as well as in view, think and analyze the landscape, sustained until then mainly by American Carl Sauer. Is worth mentioning that, for the humanist Cultural Geography, Sauer served as the basement, but did not "part of the repertoire of the work" of the humanist geographers (Marandola JR 2013: 54).

The New Cultural Geography, materialistic nature, was an important array for the formation of the current Cultural Geography, with expressive intensity in the English-speaking world (see Antipode magazine - Radical Journal of Geography, 1969).

Cosgrove, in 1983 offered a Cultural Geography Radical. It is worth mentioning that Cosgrove then entered the Anthropology ideas, bringing the concept of symbolic landscape. It was odd the question of landscape and symbolism. For him, "landscape carries multiple layers of meaning" (Cosgrove 1984: 13). The landscape is presented as symbolic form, imbued with values, not just material form.

Berque, in turn, considers the landscape as the "dimension sensible et symbolique du milieu; expression d´une médiance" (Berque 1990; 1998: 84, apud Risso 2008).

Many professionals and thinkers of humanist cultural geography, even if taken as cultural geographers, meaning that is currently advancing in the world and in Brazil. However, the renewal of Cultural Geography also provided a projection to the humanist Cultural Geography, although there is need to improve this approach with new perspectives and deepening the phenomenological method.

As for the theme, Marandola Jr. (2013: 56) states that, in Brazil, this is already happening, and the Anglo-Saxon geography, "which abandoned the term humanist geography (...) in favor of joining the cultural movement" in the mid-2000s they are returning the phenomenological project through post-phenomenological philosophy, for example, John Wylie and Mitch Rose (2006), Ash and Simpson (2014).

According to Ash e Simpson (2014: 1) there are three key elements that differentiate phenomenology from post-phenomenology:

First is a rethinking of intentionality as an emergent relation with the world, rather than an a priori condition of experience. Second is "a recognition that objects have an autonomous existence outside of the ways they appear to or are used by human beings. Third is a reconsideration of our relations with alterity, taking this as central to the constitution of phenomenological experience given our irreducible being-with the world.

About the concept of landscape of the Wylie (2007), he understands landscape in terms of tension (presence/absence; invisible/visible) "Thought this way, the term landscape names neither an external surface nor a set of cultural meanings, but rather the materialities and sensibilities with which we see" (Wylie, 2016).

Finally, the cultural geography, especially for phenomenology has significant potential for conceptual landscape debate in the patrimonial area.

2.1. Cultural geography: Contributions to the discussion of landscape as heritage

The landscape as heritage, was adopted in 1992, during the UNESCO World Heritage Convention. Nonetheless, the term has been adopted cultural landscape, comprising:

[...] Cultural landscapes are cultural properties and represent the "combined works of nature and of man" designated in Article 1 of the Convention. They are illustrative of the evolution of human society and settlement over time, under the influence of the physical constraints and/or opportunities presented by their natural environment and of successive social, economic and cultural forces, both external and internal (UNESCO 1992:1).

But the concept adopted in 2000 during the European Landscape Convention (CEP), in Florence (Italy), understands the landscape as "part of the territory, as perceived by people, whose character results from the action and interaction of factors natural and human" (Artigo 1-a- European Landscape Convention 2000).

The landscape' concepts adopted by UNESCO and the European Landscape Convention received influences of Geography ideas. In the case of UNESCO, the cultural adjective in the landscape is similar to the concept of Sauer (1998), which seeks to tell the human interaction with nature, printing marks on the natural landscape.

This observation was also made by Ribeiro (2007:112), with regard to the UNESCO subcategory on the landscape evolved organically, which "carries a very strong saueriana matrix by evolutionist and historicist perspective, emphasizing the way man has built particular landscape over time".

This type of landscape subcategory, according to Fowler (2003 apud Figueiredo 2013: 93-94) accounted for 60% of registered cultural landscapes between 1992-2002 also notable rural predominance.

This proves that the old conception of landscape is still very prevalent and, as a category, there is still criticism. This Sauer's view allows a dichotomy (nature-culture), which refers to Cultural Geography Classical, overtaken by Humanist and Cultural Geography.

Concerning the concept of the European Landscape Convention, it innovates by inserting the question of subjectivity in landscapes. Because of this singularity, many landscape settings, resulting in cultural discussions in geography, can be considered in landscape management proposals.

In Brazil, the federal institution responsible for asset protection is the IPHAN (the historical and artistic heritage Institute), which recognized the cultural landscape and set the seal only in 2009, under the decree 127 (IPHAN 2009).

According this same ordinance, Brazil's cultural landscape "is a peculiar portion of the country, representative of man's interaction process with the natural environment, to which life and human science or printed attributed values" (Article 1). In practice, the IPHAN has a more comprehensive view that UNESCO, with teams that are trying to relate the cultural and natural elements, material and immaterial.

Therefore, Geography can contribute to the heritage debate, through the presented concepts that allow us to interpret the landscape, taking into consideration people's perceptions, values and meanings in relation to landscapes. Moreover, it can contribute also with methodologies that integrate Nature and Culture. For example, if the environment perception studies, techniques involving observation, interviews and projective techniques, according Whyte (1978: 21) that allow "(...) à une population locale de rassembler de l'information à son propre, et une aptitude à la recherche au plan local" (Whyte 1978: 18).

Thus, the Cultural Geography Humanist and Cultural Geography are great geographical currents geared to value issues, both material and immaterial and significations.

3. CONCLUSIONS

In the case of the Cultural Geography and the Cultural Geography Humanist, the studies of the subjective aspects of landscape, their meanings and values can contribute, in a privileged way for the heritage debate, after all, to be heritage cultural landscapes they were valued by people. However, this appreciation of natural-cultural landscapes by UNESCO, reinforces the protection offered to "elitist" and european landscapes.

In Brazil, this "elitist vision" transpires in the first title of the country's cultural landscape by UNESCO, published in Rio de Janeiro, entitled "Carioca landscapes: between the mountain and the sea". The territorial boundaries of this landscape excludes favelas and other neighborhoods. In the Brazilian context it should be noted also that is unmatched recognition of landscapes inhabited by indigenous and traditional communities. Are 246 indigenous peoples, speaking more than 150 languages! A cultural heritage undervalued.

This means that the country can have great expressiveness in the list of World Heritage Sites to contain many live cultures (traditional cultures) that are inadequately represented.

But for make this happen, there needs to other visions, new concepts of landscape and rediscovered by managers of cultural heritage. New insights and new valuations towards Latin American countries.

NOTES

[1] Translated and published in Brazil in 1998.
[2] Brazilian translation dated 2006, as contained in the references.
[3] Brazilian translation dated 1989, as contained in the references.
[4] Brazilian translation dated 1994, as contained in the references.
[5] Brazilian translation dated 1993, as contained in the references.
[6] Brazilian translation date from 1982.
[7] Brazilian translation date from 1982.
[8] The Buttimer citations are from the article dated 1976, translated in Brazil in 1982.

BIBLIOGRAPHY

Ash, J. Simpson, P. (2014). Geography and post-phenomenology. *Progress in Human Geography*, 40 (1), pp.48-66.

Bachelard, G. (1993). *A poética do espaço*. São Paulo: Martins Fontes.

Berque, A. (1990). *Médiance de milieux em paysages*. Paris: Geographiques Reclus.

Berque, A. (1998). Paisagem-marca, Paisagem-matriz: elementos da problemática para uma geografia cultural. In: R. Corrêa and Z. Rosendahl, ed., *Paisagem, tempo e cultura*. 1st ed. Rio de Janeiro, Eduerj, pp.84-91.

Claval, P.A. (2001). *Geografia Cultural*. 2th ed. Florianópolis: Editora da UFSC.

Buttimer, Anne. (1982). Apreendendo o dinamismo do mundo vivido. In: A. Christofoletti, ed., *Perspectivas da geografia*. 1st ed. São Paulo: Difel, pp. 165-193.

Cauquelin, A. (2007). *A invenção da paisagem*. São Paulo: Martins Fontes.

Collot, M. (1990). Pontos de vista sobre a percepção das Paisagens. *Boletim de Geografia Teorética*, 20 (39), p.22- 31.

Cosgrove, Denis E. (1984). *Social formation and symbolic landscape*. London: Croom Helm.

Dardel, E. (1952). *L'Homme et la terre: nature de la realité geographique*. Paris: Presses Universitaires de France.

Dardel, E. (2011). *O homem e a terra: natureza da realidade geográfica*. (trad. Werther Holzer) São Paulo: Perspectiva.

Derrida J. (1994). *Spectres of Marx*. London: Routledge.

European Landscape Convention. (2000). PhilSchi archive. Available at: http://conventions.coe.int/Treaty/en/Treaties/Html/176.htm. [Access 28 Oct. 2014].

Figueiredo, V.G.B. (2013). O patrimônio e as paisagens: novos conceitos para velhas concepções?. *Paisagem e ambiente*, 1 (32), pp.83-118.

Heidegger, M. (1989). *Ser e Tempo*. 2v. Petrópolis: Vozes.

Holzer, W. (2008). A Geografia humanista: uma revisão. *Espaço e Cultura*. Edição comemorativa, 1993-2008, pp.137-147.

Husserl, E. (2006). *Idéias para uma fenomenologia pura e para uma filosofia fenomenológica. Introdução geral à fenomenologia pura*. Tradução de Marcio Suzuki. São Paulo: Ed. Idéias e Letras.

Ihde, D. (1993). *Postphenomenology: Essays in the postmodern context*. Evanston: Northwestern University Press.

IPHAN. (2009). *Portaria n.127 de 30 de Abril de 2009*. Estabelece a chancela da paisagem cultural brasileira. Brasília, IPHAN.

Lowenthal, D. (1982). Geografia, experiência e imaginação: em direção a uma nova epistemologia geográfica. In: A. Christofoletti, ed., *Perspectivas da geografia*. 1st ed. São Paulo: Difel, pp. 103-141.

Merleau-Ponty, M. (1994). *Fenomenologia da percepção*. Trad. de Carlos Alberto Ribeiro de Moura. São Paulo: Martins Fontes.

Nancy J.L. (1991). *Shattered love in the inoperative community*. Minneapolis MN: University of Minnesota Press.

Naveh, Z and Lieberman, A. (1984). *Landscape ecology: theory and application*. New York: Springer-Verlag.

Relph, E. (1976). *Place and placelessness*. London: Pion.

Relph, E. (1979). As bases fenomenológicas da Geografia. *Geografia*, Rio Claro, v.7, pp.1-26.

Ribeiro, R.W. (2007). *Paisagem cultural e patrimônio*. Brasília: Iphan.

Ricoeur, P. (2004). *Memory, history, forgetting*. Chicago, IL: University of Chicago Press.

Risso, L.C. (2008). Paisagens e cultura: uma reflexão teórica a partir do estudo de uma comunidade indígena amazônica. *Espaço e Cultura*, (23), pp. 67-76.

Rose, M. and Wylie, J. (2006). Animating landscape. *Environment and Planning D: Society and Space*, 24 (4), pp. 475–479.

Sauer, C.O. (1998). A morfologia da Paisagem. In: R. Corrêa and Z. Rosendahl, ed., *Paisagem, tempo e cultura*. 1st ed. Rio de Janeiro: EdUERJ, pp.12-74.

Tuan, Y.F. (1961). Thopophilia or, sudden encounter with landscape. *Landscape*. 11 (1), pp. 29-32.

Tuan, Y.F. (1976). Humanistic geography. *Annals of the association of American Geographers*. 66 (2), pp. 266-276.

Tuan, Y.F. (1980). *Topofilia: um estudo de percepção, atitudes e valores do meio ambiente*. São Paulo: Difel.

Tuan, Y.F. (1982). Geografia Humanística. In: A. Christofoletti, ed, *Perspectivas da Geografia*. 1st ed. São Paulo: DIFEL, pp. 143-164.

Tuan, Y.F. (1983). *Espaço e Lugar: a Perspectiva da Experiência*. São Paulo, DIFEL.

UNESCO. (1992). Expert group on cultural landscapes. *Guidelines on the inscription of specific types of properties on the World heritage list*. La Petite Pierre, France.

Wagner, P.L. and Mikesell, M.W. (2003). Os temas da geografia cultural. In: R. Corrêa and Z. Rosendahl, ed., *Introdução à Geografia Cultural*. 1st ed. Rio de Janeiro: Bertrand Brasil, pp. 27-61.

Whyte, A.V.T. (1978). *La perception de l'environnement: lignes directrices méthodologiques pour les études sur le terrain*. UNESCO.

Wylie, J. (2007). *Landscape: key ideas in geography*. London: Routledge.

Wylie, J. (2016). *Professor John Wylie Head of Geography, and Professor of Cultural Geography*. Available at: http://geography.exeter.ac.uk/staff/index.php?web_id=John_Wylie&tab=research. [Access 20 Jan. 2016].

THE IMAGE OF THE COUNTRYSIDE.
THEORETICAL AND METHODOLOGICAL APPROACH

Paulina Tobiasz-Lis
Department of Regional and Social Geography, University of Łódź

ABSTRACT

The paper discusses the problem of social perception and images of the countryside, which seems to be marginalized in contemporary geographical research. The scientific interest in the spatial experience and perceptions is focused mainly on urban areas. Therefore, the title of the article intentionally refers to the work by Kevin Lynch (1960).
In the first place, theoretical basis of the research on rural imagery will be introduced. Then two different methods: (1) the "classical" analysis and classification of freehand sketches and (2) "innovative" photographic essays which can be used in studies of the subjective image of the countryside will be presented. In the last part, the paper will discuss examples of sketches and photographic essays of selected villages in Poland showing both designative and appraisive aspects of rural imagery and their cognitive and practical goals in studies of relations between people and their life space.

Keywords
Spatial perception, image, countryside, visual methods, freehand sketches, photographic essays

1. INTRODUCTION

The last 30 years in social sciences represent a real theoretical and methodological revolution, manifested above all by the interest in culture in different contexts and dimensions. All the transformations that took place in this period are often described as 'cultural changes'. The number of undertaken research problems by the culture scientists (anthropologists, sociologists, geographers) is so huge, that it is difficult to create transparent classification of such studies. The common denominator for most works is the reference to everyday life, as a specific interpretation of character of the social life. Different areas of knowledge 'uncover' and interpret everyday life in relations to its different symptoms. One of them is looking for meanings, which are assigned by people in the process of perception and structuring their surrounding reality in the light of their culture and experience (Rose 2001: 20). The key element of conscious process of accustoming reality by people is the visual sphere. The character of images that surround us and their social perception is, according to many scientists, an important element of the cultural process for constructing social life of the Western civilization and constitutes an element for wider analysis of the society transformation from pre-modernity to modernity, and later from modernity to post-modernity (Rose 2001: 20-21). Images carry information, knowledge, emotions, aesthetic feelings, values. According to P. Sztompka (2005), we can read them as a text.

The aim of the following article is to interpret the image of the countryside remembered in the consciousness of inhabitants and reproduced in a form of freehand sketches and photographic essays. The issue of perception and space images was initiated and developed mostly in cities. Regardless of the aspect of undertaken research for experiences and spatial remembering, works referring to the social perception of space in the countryside appeared later and were rather seldom. The 'cultural change' in geographic research of the rural areas was connected most of all with British works in the 90-ties of last century. Geographers started then to consider the dimensions of 'rurality' and tried to put them in the context of traditional terms. That research concentrated on processes co-creating current meaning of 'rurality' especially different forms of spatial practices, which characterize the rural style of life (Woods 2011).

Freehand sketches and photographic essays of the countryside presented and interpreted in this article are examples of social representations of the countryside, in other words colloquial and institutionalized forms of knowledge and construction of the countryside, which beside rural locality practices, that is behaviours and activities with the local dimension and everyday lives, i.e. forms of popular discussion concerning countryside and specific experiencing of its space, are the concept element of 'threefold complexity' of rural space K. Halfacree (2004), being the expression of contemporary multi-dimensional understanding of 'countryside' and 'rurality'. Space in the perspective of social representations is experienced everyday and is subject to structuration in human minds, according to guidelines of social constructivism. Both the sketch of close space (in case of the countryside this is mainly the neighbourhood space) and the individual relations in the form of photographic essay are full of symbols, expressing meanings, but also values attributed to specific places.

1.1. Methodology

The pioneer for research concerning space images was K. Lynch (1960), who developed and applied the method of freehand sketch analyses – a graphic form of reconstructing knowledge concerning space based in the most part on visual perception. According to K. Lynch (1960: 131), 'Shaping spatial images is a dual process between the observer and the observing object. What the observer notices is an external form, but the way it is interpreted and paid attention to this form, influences what the observer really sees'. Besides the issue of attribute of space allowing their easy identification by a human being, K. Lynch (1960) paid great attention to the meanings of individual places and objects being the effect of their practical and emotional evaluation. On the basis of research carried out in three cities: Boston, New Jersey and Los Angeles, he distinguished five elements of urbanized space structure, which make up its image, that is:

1. Paths are channels, that the people move along. These can be streets, sidewalks, bicycle paths or railway lines. In the image structure of many people this is the dominant element because they observe the city while moving along these paths, whereas the remaining elements are added to the sketches and remain in close spatial relation with the paths.

2. Nodes are objects, which can be entered, or which constitute strategic points serving navigation and orientation in the city. These could be street crossings, roundabouts, transit points in public transport, bus or tram terminus. Nodes can be significant 'events' while moving along paths, therefore their concept is strongly connected to the concept of the first element distinguished by the author. At the same time, they often indicate the centre of areas, therefore their role is very significant in the shape of physical perception of the city.

3. Edges most often constitute some kind of barrier, space limitations or distances between areas, though in some cases they connect with each other. These are most often waterfronts, walls, railway dykes, rivers.

4. Areas constitute medium or large units with individual character distinguished in the city space. Besides paths, they are the second element, which can dominate sketches prepared by respondents. According to the writer of the method, this depends not only on the individual features, but also on the city space.

5. Landmarks are, similar to nodes, waypoints used in navigation in the city. Usually they are constituted by buildings, signs or other urban details, which fill up imagination of most users of the city space. Part of them can have a local character, part – especially, if they tower over the buildings of the whole city thanks to their size, determines the perceptive dominant – and become a symbol.

Analyses of freehand sketches presented by K. Lynch (1960) initiated so called structural aspect for research of city space imagination connected with their physical structure as well as relations of subjective image with reality. Both quantitative as well as qualitative analyses were subject to: content, internal structure and style of sketches, but also their spatial range and orientation according to the directions of the world. K. Lynch (1960) indicated two elementary features in the landscape of the city significant to the creation of images, therefore also for the creation of sketches: 1) legibility, which means ease, with which respective parts of the city are recognized and organized in consistent picture and 2) imagebility – specific feature of the city combining physical-spatial elements with events in the social life and personal experiences of people taking place in these or on these elements (Lynch 1960).

The analyses method of freehand sketches of K. Lynch (1960) was broadened with the proposal of their classification by D. Appleyard (1970). On the basis of analyses for the sketches structure and their level of accuracy, he arranged sketches in groups according to similarity and in sub-groups according to other specific features. In this way he distinguished the linear and spatial type. Sketches with the dominance of linear elements (paths, nodes, edges), were divided into fragmented, chained, branch and loop and netted. Among sketches with the dominance of spatial elements (landmarks, areas) he distinguished scattered, mosaic, linked sketches as well as a map (Fig. 1).

Elements of the image of city space structure distinguished by K. Lynch (1960) and the attempt to

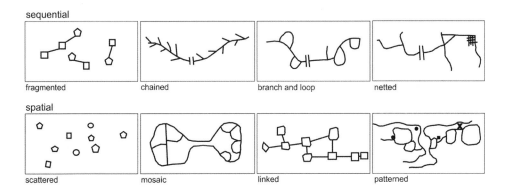

Fig.1. Types of sketch maps according to D. Appleyard (1970).

classify freehand sketches proposed by D. Appleyard are the most commonly applied in later elaborates, though they are not the only ones. Another proposal of sketch types was presented by F. C. Ladd (1970). The author did not ask respondents to draw the whole city, but only the area around the place where they live, neighbourhood. As a result she obtained sketches with much lower range, but at the same time much more detailed and often much more resembling the drawing, which presents the typical city landscape rather than a map. Among the sketches of the neighbourhood, F. C. Ladd (1970) distinguished the following four types:

1. pictorial drawings, which most often presented street;

2. schematic drawings, which included information about streets, areas, but the way of presentation was rather general;

3. drawings resembling map, which could serve as a map and help in the orientation on a particular area, but included a small number of elements;

4. maps with landmarks, which allowed to recognize the neighbourhood and could help to find yourself in the area (Fig.2).

It seems that besides different classification of freehand sketches, which resulted from the various

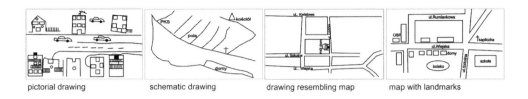

| pictorial drawing | schematic drawing | drawing resembling map | map with landmarks |

Fig.2. Types of sketch maps according to F. C. Ladd (1970).

scale of mapped fragments of space by the respondents, the content of imaginative maps in all cases refers to the proposal of K. Lynch (1960), so it is possible to distinguish paths, landmarks, nodes, areas and edges in them, which make up the image of a structure for specific fragment of space – no matter if the whole city was drawn or just a part of it. **The following elaborate presents an attempt for analyses and interpretation of freehand sketches of the countryside invoking to the image elements distinguished by K. Lynch (1960) and, due to the scale of researched settlement units, classification of neighbourhood sketches proposed by F. C. Ladd (1970).**

Images of the countryside in the form of freehand sketches were collated with the image of countryside space presented in photographic essays, prepared by inhabitants in a few villages in the Łódź province. Every essay constituted identification of places with different, determined in advance characteristics, i.e.: 'beautiful place', 'ugly place', 'place, which tells the story of the countryside', 'place, which creates positive emotions', 'place, which creates negative emotions', 'place, where the time passes slowly', 'place, where the time passes fast' and 'my place', which determination was left to the people preparing the essays. Photographs of certain places were accompanied by explanations of their choices in the form of short descriptions. According to Y.-F. Tuan (1987) 'places constitute centres of sensed values'. The collection of significant places, connected with granting the space a symbolic dimension in the individual as well as collective sense makes up the notion of cultural space in contemporary human geography (Lisowski 2003).

Research conducted in Japan, among others (Noda 1988; Hisa and Utsumi 1992, Teramoto and Ohnishi 1995, after: Okamato 2006), with the use of so called „photo projective method", concentrated mostly on children, who were given photo cameras and were asked to photograph cities in general, or specific places – those liked or not liked. T. Okamato and others (2006) asked students from one of the Japanese universities to photograph places characteristic on the grounds of the campus and those, which are not characteristic and to justify their choice. Similar research concerning evaluation of the space of the whole city was conducted in Łódź (Tobiasz-Lis, Wójcik 2013). Among numerous advantages of this method for people taking part in research, most often was emphasized the ease and the possibility of individual interpretation of space while taking photographs, which is difficult to reach during standard social surveys. At the same time, the results showed, that besides subjectiveness of feelings and assessment of individual people, as well as the ease given by the photographic method, most images can be interpreted as an illustration of typical impressions, average for all the participants of the survey.

Research of space features, where photographs were used, assumed that they constitute image of relations between the photographer and the surrounding space, therefore the researcher can try to interpret subjective images and meaning of individual places in their individual and collective contents. Similar behaviour was presented in the analyses of freehand sketches before. According to concepts for perception of space formulated in the geographical research (Saarinen 1969; Bartnicka 1989), firstly – there is an objective, external world in relations to an individual, secondly – there is a separate, subjective entity mind and thirdly – there is a possibility to discover sensual-mental world, known as image.

2. THE COUNTRYSIDE FROM THE PERSPECTIVE OF FREEHAND SKETCHES
AND INDIVIDUAL PHOTOGRAPHIC ESSAYS

Research concerning images of space with the use of freehand sketches method was conducted in eleven villages located in Łódź, Masovia and Małopolska provinces, which were characterised by diverse genesis, physiognomy and functions performed. Selection of people participating in the research had a quota character. It was attempted to retain proportions of elementary socio-demographic features of the population of individual settlements, such as: age, sex and education. A small number of respondents – several people in every village, was justified for the reason of the elementary target of conducted research, which is the initial exploration of phenomena, as well as its qualitative character (Babbie 2004). Inhabitants were asked to prepare freehand sketches of the village in a way that would present surrounding, including the most important elements of space according to them. Below, example sketches of the village of Babiczki, Podgórzyce and Sacin were presented and described..

Irrespective of the character and specific features of individual villages, and the socio-demographic features of people taking part in the conducted research, their images in the form of freehand sketches of the nearest area take different form and can be classified to all types, which were distinguished and described in literature by F. C. Ladd (1970) – starting from pictorial, presenting only the most important parts of the settlement, and finishing with maps with orientation points, which reflected whole villages, indicating and naming neighbouring areas at the same time.

Types of village sketches, their shape, structure and content can be interpreted in the context of two fundamental issues – 1) size, character of development and functions of the village, especially the quality of social infrastructure and 2) strategy for making sketches adapted by individual people participating in the research. In the first case – the bigger diversification, the richer images, taking the shape of expanded schematic sketches, sketches resembling a map or maps with landmarks. In the case of strategy for drawing up sketches we should refer to the classification of imaginative maps of G. Rand (1969 after: Mordwa 2003), who distinguished sketches of 'taxi driver' type – presenting fragments of space, including unoriented sets of roads resulting from everyday, individual experiences – in this case the main road in the village and the most important objects located along, as well as sketches of the 'aeroplane pilot' type – more abstract and internally integrated, covering in this case bigger parts or even whole villages.

Sketches of all villages, irrespective of the represented type, were started from the main road, along which the settlement was developing. Depending on the size of the village, one or several streets were taken into account, nevertheless concentrating mostly on objects with important social functions, i.e.: churches, wayside shrines, cemeteries, schools, bus stops, fire depots. It was these elements that dominated in all images of villages. Besides the network of roads and significant landmarks, sketches included also living areas, often highlighting own place of living or houses belonging to relatives. Interestingly, especially in the perspective of contemporary socio-economic changes of the Polish countryside, it seems rather rare to draw farmlands, which appeared only in every tenth sketch and mostly served the function of 'filling' the empty space on the checker (Fig. 5b).

The range of spatial sketches is diversified – the smallest one characterises sketches covering those parts of the village with important objects – church, school, wayside shrine, where inhabitants meet, spend time together, make friendships and care for neighbourhood relationships (Fig. 4a). Schematic sketches, which resemble a map or maps with landmarks, have a much wider range, often including names of neighbouring areas and indicate their location in regard to mapped villages (Fig. 4b, 5b).

Structure, order of drawn elements and the spatial range of village sketches are different from the sketches described in literature, which are prepared by inhabitants of cities. Urban areas are characterised by much bigger complexity of forms, functions and meanings, and their users experience usually only selected parts of cities, which is reflected by the character of their images. Sketches of cities, depending on the accepted drawing strategy, are started by inhabitants from drawing own place of living and the closest surrounding (then the range of the sketch covers part of the city, but includes more details) or from the central surrounding, that have a representative meaning, and filled with elements of symbolic meaning – both in the collective perspective, as well as individual meanings (then the range of the sketch covers more often the whole city, but included elements are generalised) (Tobiasz-Lis 2013).

On the other hand, differentiation of sketch orientation of the countryside results from several factors, which were also paid attention to in image research conducted with the use of this method in cities (Mordwa 2003; Tobiasz-Lis 2013), among others:

1. from the occurrence of characteristic objects in the village space, which make orientation easier, e.g. church, road and building system, pond (Fig. 5);

2. from the range of the spatial sketch – the bigger, the more often characteristic elements of spatial structure are included and it is oriented to the north side;

3. from the place of living of the person drawing the sketch, which influences the perspective and directions representing everyday experience of space included in the sketch (Fig. 3).

Analyses of the presented countryside sketches confirms, that the perception of space consists in the first place in identification, that is recognising the components of environment and distinguishing some elements from others, their structuralization, that is defining the spatial relation between components of environment as well as on evaluation, that is defining meanings of individual elements for the perceived entity.

The countryside represented by the inhabitants in photographic essays constitutes significant deepening of space images included in freehand sketches and allows for more comprehensive interpretation of meanings given and read in specific places as a result of their everyday experiencing. Some parts of the village become more clear, readable, create both positive and negative emotions among inhabitants, which is the basis for their evaluation. Photographic essays constitute an image of individual 'micro worlds' and reports, that connect inhabitants of the village with important places and objects for them, where their lives and the lives of all local communities revolves around and is organized. In the interpretation of individual places it is possible to feel harmonious coexistence of the human world, natural world and things strengthened in rural areas, which was also mentioned in the research of kieleckie countryside by E. Szot-Radziszewska (2013).

Below you can find correlated parts of one of the photographic essays of Popielawy village, located in Rokiciny commune, in the Tomaszów district, in Łódź province. Among others, such parts were chosen, which not only referred to specific places and their meaning for the author of the essay, but also to the

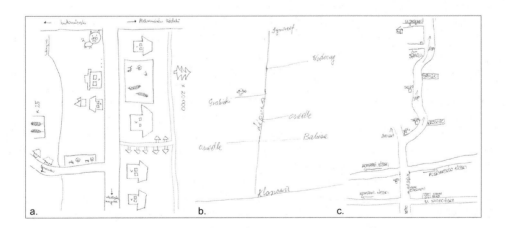

Fig.3. Examples of sketch maps of the Babiczki village (Nowe Miasto nad Pilicą commune, Grójec district, Masovia province) a. pictorial drawing, b. schematic drawing, c. map with landmarks.

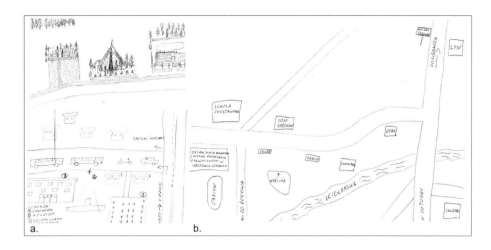

Fig.4. Examples of sketch maps of the Kaczki Średnie village (Turek commune, Turek district, Wielkopolska province) a. pictorial drawings, b. map with landmarks.

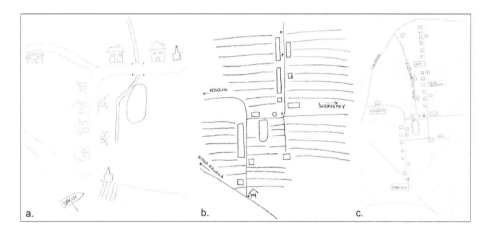

Fig.5. Examples of sketch maps of the Sacin village (Nowe Miasto nad Pilicą commune, Grójec district, Masovia province) a. pictorial drawing, b. schematic drawing, c. map with landmarks.

experienced time, which similar to space, is a natural aspect of human existence. Human being not only stays in a particular length of time, but time temporalizes in the life of human being and in the human culture.

Place, which tells the story of a village: *"this is the only wooden cross in the neighbourhood. It was made from the larch wood in 1825. At the beginning of the 20th century the whole village was hit by cholera. (...) Many people died then. The only hope was in God. (...) Villagers, as a gratitude to God for saving their lives, decided to construct a cross, which was to symbolise a new beginning. The villagers still care for the cross. It is still decorated with flowers. The story of the disease is carried along".*

Place, which creates positive emotions: *"Family home is a special place for everyone. It is connected with many memories. I always feel safe and happy there. With time I observe as everything is changing around, but the house remains the same. (...) I am happy to be living away from noise, close to a quiet road and beautiful neighbourhood".*

67

Place, which inspires us: *"my grandfather is a beekeeper. He looks after them all year round. You have to take great cafe about those hard working insects. They require much attention, so that you can collect the first honey already in spring. I admire bees, their hard work and organization skills. Such small creatures, yet they are able to collect nectar from flowers and transform it in delicious and healthy honey. I like to come to the garden and watch my grandfather looking after them. It is really incredible, how the are able to cooperate with each other. Thanks to them and my grandfather's work I can always count on fresh honey."*

Place, where time passes quickly: *"For me field is a place, where time definitely seems to speed up. While working, we suddenly come to a conclusion, that an hour or two have passed. Sometimes there is no time to rest and you have to work fast, because the rain is coming. At that time everybody is trying hard to do all without checking the time."*

Place, where time passes slowly: *"For many years I used to travel to school in Łódź. I always waited for a coach or a minibus. No matter if it snowed or rained I had to go. Unfortunately the waiting time for transport was long, and the bus never came according to the schedule."*

Place, where time stands still: *"The windmill koźlak was built between 1947-48.After 4 years it was transformed into a mil, and such is its function until today. Presently it is in private hands. The mil is moved by an electric engine, and its production capacity was increased from 1.7 tones to 4 tones of grain per day. It produces mainly so called 'razówka' and sharps for animals. As far as I remember it looked the same. As a child I often watched the whole process of making flour. To this day nothing has changed. The mil resembles old times but it is still fully operational."*

place evolving good feelings-home

place where time passes fast-farmland

place telling the story of the village-wayside cross

place which inspires me-hives

place where time passes slowly-bus stop

place where the time stopped - the mill

Fig.6. Places included in photographic essay presentin Popielawy village
(Rokiciny commune, Tomaszów Mazowiecki district, Łódź province). Compiled by author.

3. CONCLUSIONS

Freehand sketches and photographic essays presenting spatial image of the countryside have great meaning in the research of human life environment. As forms of the world structuring in the human mind, they fulfil many cognitive and practical functions – broadening the perspective of research with the issue of subjective space. Sketches and photographic essays of the countryside allow to determine not only the character of images (form), but it is also possible to describe contemporary nature of the 'countryside' and its aspect thanks to included contents.

The cognitive function refers most of all to the interpretation of the countryside as a certain territory, where the social processes take place. Fundamental difference in shaping the social environment of the countryside in relation to the urban environment depends on the key role of neighbourhood in the reproduction of interpersonal relationships. In this case , the scale is important, which refers to the image of material structure (morphology or structure of the countryside) as well as the character of the relation between human and the environment, which is greatly based on the functional and social relationships between the 'middle' (in this case it is mostly the family home) and subsequent spheres of surrounding mainly responsible for closer and farther neighbourhood.

The functional aspect includes the usefulness of environment and the ways of connecting individual spaces ('places') being the subject of everyday experiences. Village people, through sketch or photographs, show essentially forms of inhabiting the countryside (its homogeneousness or diversification), so that it is possible to conclude about the coherence or its lack in the architectural-landscape dimension. Connectivity is by contrast not only the function of homestead, farmhouse, allotment border, but mainly it is expressed by the image of common or public space and different types of institutions (traffic function) included in it.

The social aspect covers mostly the sphere of symbolism, which already results from the choice, and next, in the case of a sketch, from the size and the level of generalization of certain elements. Institutions included in sketches or presented in essays should be than treated mainly as emanation of community life. They inform us about the methods of social communication, and thanks to it we can obtain knowledge not only concerning the way of subjective reflection of space, but we also learn a lot about the sketcher and his/her connection with the countryside.

Practical aspect of this way to research contemporary countryside has a big connection with planning the countryside, especially in the conditions its quick desagrarization. Sketches make us realize largely the disappearance of productive function of the countryside, and thereby the marginalization of the expanse role in shaping functional and social relations. The correct planning of the countryside should include the role of nature in creating rusticity. Harmony in the countryside environment is the result of interactions between human and nature, which have different background (productive and non-productive). In order to retain the specificity of the countryside it is important to plan open areas, which should serve the contemporary society in the same way as expanses before in sustaining biological needs (production of food) and social needs of the rural inhabitants. That is why it is significant to plan such functions of the countryside, which character will include forms of social practises referring to surface development. In this case sketches can appear to be very helpful, especially on the stage of identifying elementary problems of planning local development connected with the issue of weakening social relationships, or imagery and readability of elements for the spatial structure of the countryside, which are the sign of dynamic changes of contemporary world. We obtain therefore information on the subject of quality of everyday life space of individual people, places important both from the perspective of individual experiences and from the experiences of all local communities.

Inhabitants taking part in the conducted research paid attention to the fact that both drawing a sketch and preparing a photographic essay allowed them to observe more closely the surrounding space and everyday life of their community. From the research perspective, obtained images of countryside in this way constitute recording and perpetuation of certain visual facts in a specific time-space context, illustrate concepts, categories and regularity of social reality, but are also a heuristic inspiration and a base for wider interpretation of social space and cultural scenery.

NOTES

Presented research is a part of National Science Centre funding scheme, "Spatial representations of rural settlements in Poland" conducted by the Department of Regional and Social Geography, University of Łódź since the spring of 2015.

BIBLIOGRAPHY

Appleyard, D. (1970). Styles and methods of structuring a city. *Environment and Behaviour*, No. 2, pp. 100-117.

Babbie, E. (2004). *Badania społeczne w praktyce*. Wydawnictwo Naukowe PWN, Warszawa.

Bartnicka, M. (1989). Wyobrażenia przestrzeni miejskiej Warszawy – studium geografii percepcji. *Dokumentacja Geograficzna*, no 2.

Halfacree, K. (2004). Rethinking 'Rurality', In: Champion T., Graeme H. (eds.), *New Form of Urbanization. Beyond the Urban-Rural Dichotomy*. Ashgate, Burlington, pp. 285-306

Ladd, F. C. (1970). Black youths view their environment: neighborhood maps. *Environment and Behaviour*, no 2, pp. 74-99.

Lisowski, A. (2003). *Koncepcje przestrzeni w geografii człowieka*, Uniwersytet Warszawski, Warszawa.

Lynch, K. (1960). *The image of the city*. MIT Press Cambridge.

Mordwa, S. (2003). *Wyobrażenia miast Polski Środkowej*. Wydawnictwo Uniwersytetu Łódzkiego, Łódź.

Okamoto, T., Fujihara, T., Kato, J., Kosugi, K., Nakazato, N., Hayashi, Y., Ikeuchi, H., Nakagawa, N. Mori and K., Nonami, H. (2006), Measuring social stereotypes with the photo projective method. *Social Behaviour and Personality*. 34(3). pp. 319-332.

Rose, G. (2001). *Visual Methodologies: An Introduction to Interpreting Visual Materials*. Sage.

Saarinen, T. F. (1969). *Perception of the environment*. Washington, Association of American Geographers, Commission on College Geography Resource, Paper 5.

Szot-Radziszewska, E. (2013). *Obraz wsi w wyobrażeniach mieszkańców. Miejsca i ludzie*. Wydawnictwo Politechniki Świętokrzyskiej, Kielce.

Sztompka, P. (2005). *Socjologia wizualna. Fotografia jako metoda badawcza*. Wydawnictwo Naukowe PWN, Warszawa.

Tobiasz-Lis, P. (2013). *Zmiany wyobrażeń mieszkańców Łodzi o przestrzeni miasta*. Wydawnictwo Uniwersytetu Łódzkiego, Łódź.

Tobiasz-Lis, P. Wójcik, M. (2013). Evaluating and interpreting the city using a photo projective method. The example of Lodz. *Geographia Polonica*, 86(2), IG&SO PAS, pp. 137-152.

Tuan, Y.F. (1987). *Przestrzeń i miejsce*, Państwowy Instytut Wydawniczy, Warszawa.

THE INTERACTION BETWEEN LANDSCAPE AND ART. PARKS OF MEMORY AND MUSEUM PARKS

Beata Makowska
Cracow University of Technology, Faculty of Architecture, Division of Freehand Drawing,
Painting and Sculpture

ABSTRACT

The paper presents selected parks and gardens associated with natural landscape which surrounds them, the history of places and people living there. Parks of memory constitute a kind of sculpture gallery in the open air. They also unite open and built space, emphasizing landscape and local cultural values. Owing to places for recreation and cultural events they became attractive public space for residents and tourists. Gardens located in the neighbourhood of museums and art galleries are integrally connected with the collections, serving an important role in their promotion. The integration of gardens and museums appeals new visitors to them, it has educational values as well. It creates cultural models and increases attractiveness of public spaces in a crowded cities. Based on the examples presented in the paper we can draw a conclusion that the interaction between landscape and art influence a protection of regional identity and traditional elements of the environment. Gardens and parks are developing awareness of the existing values, shaping perception of space and increasing sensitivity for art. They are also considerably contributing to formation of cultural models and mechanisms.

Keywords
parks of memory, museum parks, art gallery gardens

1. INTRODUCTION

The paper presents selected parks and gardens associated with natural landscape which surrounds them, the history of places and people living there i.e. parks of memory, parks designed close to the museums. Such parks constitute a kind of sculpture gallery in the open air and city parks. They unite open and built space, emphasizing landscape and local cultural values. Owing to places for recreation and cultural events they became attractive public space for residents and tourists.

The research method adopted is the combination of the *in situ* study and the data taken from the published literature and online publications concerning the examples of parks and gardens presented in the paper.

2. THE PARK DES PERSONNALITÉS IN HONFLEUR

An interesting example is the park des Personnalités, opened in 2004 in Honfleur (France), created in area of estuary of Seine (Fig. 1-2). It is devoted to memory of the outstanding persons associated with local history (artists, writers and other great personalities), whose busts located in separately designed parts of the park are commemorating them. The curved sculptures of 19 personnes represent: navigators (Binot Paulmier de Gonneville, Samuel de Champlain, Jean Doublet, Pierre Berthelot), historical personalities

(Charles V, Jean-Baptiste Colbert, Anne-Marie Louis d'Orléans), painters (Claude Monet, Eugène Boudin, Johan Bartold Jonkind, Léon Leclerc, Alexandre Dubourg), poets (Charles Baudelaire), composers (Erik Satie) and other artists (writer Alphonse Allais; journalist, writer and sculptor Lucie Delarue Mardrus; writer Marie Catherine d'Aulnoy). The busts of writer Françoise Sagan and actor Michel Serrault were also added in 2010.They have spent a part of their life in Honfleur. A picturesque landscape of a Norman waterside attracted now-bust-commemorated artists. Its unique light and colours inspired their work.

The park, which has an area of 10 hectares, connects Honfleur to the sea with the shore marking out the park's compositional frames. Open space, small lake and the neighbouring sea create rest-favouring

Fig.1. The park des Personnalités in Honfleur (photo by B. Makowska, 2014).

Fig.2. The park des Personnalités in Honfleur (photo by B. Makowska, 2014).

ambience. They repeat the lines', rhythms' and forms' arrangement which is present in the natural landscape. Views of a town, port and the surrounding landscape are used in the composition of specific frames and fragments. Certain parts of the park, mingling and connecting one with another into a coherent composition in the open space, encourage promenades. Boat-shaped hedges symbolise not only the time which has elapsed and the history of the local community, but also do they symbolise the future and the desire for artistic continuation. Michel Lamare (the Mayor of Honfleur in 2004), the initiator of the creation of the park, coined the idea that: "knowing your past enables you to understand the present and prepare yourself for the future" (information written on a board in the park).

The sculpture park in Honfleur is an example of a project using elements of the exitsisng landscape and new forms which relate to the history of the town. It is an important factor in shaping the awareness of the past and creating new perspectives for the citizens' modern daily life. The park contributes to the creation of a continuity, both in the perspective of the landscape and the town, as well as its history. Park also plays an essential role in the children's education for they can discover great historical personas and local artists (each bust has a description in French and English of the person portrayed). Perhaps visiting the park will awaken their curiosity to learn the town's history.

The are numerous cultural events taking place in the park i.e. Le Pique Nique Musical (2014), in which children from local school (l'École de Musique de Honfleur) were participated [1]. It is also a place to expose and highlight current work of the local artists. These actions help not only to promote the town and increase its touristic value but also, indirectly, economic growth of the Basse Normandie region.

Nowadays, on the opposite estuary of the Seine close to the Pont de Normandie, The Parc d'Activités Calvados Honfleur is being built (the project is designed by: Aktis Architecture, la Compagnie du Paysage; 2007-2017). It is inspired by eco-industrial projects made in Canada, USA and Portugal. These projects use renewable energy. Park creates an eco passage which will be multifunctional for the "new generation". This park, which has an area of 130 hectares, located between Honfleur and port in Havre, second largest in the Rouen region, will protect the region from uncontrolled industrial development and its negative influence on the environment.

3. THE LIVSGLEDE PARK IN BRYNE

An interesting example is also the Livsglede park (opened in 2004) in Bryne (Norway) designed in the form of walkway along the river with sculptures of the local artist Fritz Røed(1929-2002). Ten of his sculptures were made from bronze and entitled: Small Sunday Princess, Leaping Centaur, Calm, Protection, Pierrot, Carnevale in Venice, Klaun and Circus Dog, Memento Mori and journalist Arne Garborg. A sculpture of a lapwing completes the collection; it was made by Røeda's friend, Waksvika, by the sculptor's sketch. This bird is there for a special reason as it appears on the town's coat-of-arms. Usually-vertical sculptures were contrasted to the horizontally formed plants, consciously juxtaposting their textures (Fig. 3-4). The elements inspired by natural Norwegian landscape were used at the end of the compositional axis in this park (waterfall, lake, hytte).

Park "A song about life" (Livsglede) extracts local cultural and landscape values, and unites the space of Bryne – a small Norwegian town located in 2001. It serves as an opportunity to present and popularise work of the local sculptors, as well as to remember the artists and to protect their works of art for the future generations (Makowska 2012: 203-208). It also contributes to shaping the audience's sensitivity. Humorous sculptures attract the youngest and encourage them play one with another.

The are numerous cultural events taking place in the park i.a. workshops, concerts and the Fritz Røed festival entitled „Joy of Life Festival", organised each yearch at the beginning of March. During festivals, a variety of delicious food is served, and a detailed program of cultural events is prepared. Needless to say that this place became an important social area, integrating the local community [2].

Fig.3. The Livsglede park in Bryne (photo by B. Makowska, 2010).

Fig.4. The Livsglede park in Bryne (photo by B. Makowska, 2010).

4. THE SCULPTURE GARDEN AT THE PEGGY GUGGENHEIM COLLECTION IN VENICE

An interesting collection of contemporary sculturesis exhibited in the garden at the Peggy Guggenheim Collection in Venice. The art collection was created in 1976 and began displayed to the public in 1951 (seasonally only in Summer, since 1985 it has been open year-round). Giuseppe Marchiori was a curator at this art gallery. In 1976 Peggy Guggenheim had donated the Palazzo Venier dei Leoni and the collection of art to the Salomon Guggenheim Foundation. Since then it has been enlarged by new pieces of art i.e. American and European art of 70-ties and 80-ties, donated by Hannelore B. Schulhof.Outside the gallery the Patsy R. and Raymond D. Nasher Sculpture Garden presents works from the permanent collections, which authors are famous sculptors, including works by Anish Kapoor, Isamu Noguchi, Anthony Caro, Barbara Hepworth, Jenn Holzer, Hans Arp, Henry Moore, Max Ernst, Raymond Duchami-Villon, Marino Marini and Sol LeWitt. It presents also sculptures on temporary loan from private collections and foundations (i.e. Jene Highstein Anish Kapoor, Marino Marini, Maurizio Nannucci).

The gallery became a popular tourist destination, visible from Grand Canal during a vaporetto and boat journey. The sculptures have been brilliantly combined with the plants, harmonising their form and texture very well. Many of the works of art are very often used as a background for the photographs, what creates an interaction between the art and the people, i.e. scuplture – distorting mirror (Fig. 5). There are also special cultural events organised in the art gallery, garden and on the Roof Tarrace i.e. children and families educational programmes, internships for students who study art and art history [3].

5. THE MUSÉE DU QUAI BRANLY AND THE MUSEUM OF MIDDLE AGES IN PARIS

The paper also presents gardens located in the neighbourhood of museums in Paris (the Musée du Quai Branly, the Museum of Middle Ages). These gardens are integrally connected with museum collections, serving an important role in their promotion. The integration of gardens and museums appeals new visitors to them, it has educational values as well. It creates cultural models and increases attractiveness of public spaces in a crowded cities (Makowska 2010: 179-188).These gardens, in their subject matter, resemble the museum collection, carrying it over into the town's space. They are a scenographic background to the museum collection, what makes them worth visiting.

The Musée du Quai Branly was designed by Agency Jean Nouvel, Françoise Raynaud, Isabelle Guillauic, Didier Brault in 2006. In its exhibitions, displays, inter alia, naïve art from Asia, Oceania, Africa, North America and South America. The garden surrounding the museum, with a characteristic tall grass, was made to resemble the natural environment, evoking associations of open space, untouched by the mankind (Fig 6). Jean Nouvel has labled it a "holy forest" [4]. The garden which has an area of 1,8

Fig.5. The Sculpture Garden at the Guggenheim Collection in Venice (photo by B. Makowska, 2014).

hectares was designed by Gilles Clément. One of the museum's elevations is also covered with greenery, which has 200 meters of lenth and 12 meters of hight. The vertical garden designed by Patric Blanc has characteristics found in the French gardens – geometric boundaries, in this case marked out by the edges of the walls and the building's windows [5].

The garden at the Museum of Middle Ages which has an area 5000 square meters, was designed in 2000 by Éric Ossart i Arnaud Maurières [6]. This project, inspired by the medieval order, was based on historic documents and gobelins from the plant-themed museum collection (mainly medicinal and aromatic plants). They reconstructed the Hortus Conclusus ambience with the characteristic closed, private and bounded spaces; however, they did not create the exact copy of a medieval garden.

The garden's composition is created by square and rectangular flowebeds and lawns with geometrically-ordered paths. Plants in each of the separated parts were divided into four groups [7]. The first one, edible garden, or a so called kitchen garden (i.e. cabbage, garlic, onion, chive), is inspired by the 14th century textbook for young wives entitled *Ménagier de Paris*. The second one, medical garden, features herbs with medicinal properties (i.e. mint, sage, medical verbena). The third one, dedicated to the Virgin Mary (the celestial garden), features, inter alia, lilies, irises, violets and roses – red, symbolising suffering and white, symbolising virginity. The last one is named the garden of love, with neatly trimmed spruces and violets and daisies growing in the grass (*topiary*). The quarters are separated with wooden balustrades, flooring and benches encouraging people to sit on them (Fig. 7). All this enables the visitors to have a closer contact with the plants, to inhale their scent. One of the garden's parts called "unicorn forest" features trees overgrown with ivy. In its neighbourhood, there is a place where one can rest and a playground for children with animal-shaped swings. On the flooring, there are tracks of a lion, a rabbit, a fox and a unicorn – animals which appear on the gobelins in the museum collection. Even the lady from the gobelin imprinted her palm in the flooring. Innovative forms such as fountain with mirrors (the Fontaine aux roseaux d'argent designed by Brigitte Nahon) were used in the garden at the Museum of Middle Ages next to the museum, referring to the convex mirrors from the museum collection (Białonowska 2007: 245). This place became a great spot to display works of the contemporary artists.

Fig.6. The Musée du Quai Branly in Paris (photo by B. Makowska, 2009).

Fig.7. The Museum of Middle Ages in Paris (photo by B. Makowska, 2009).

The parisian gardens mentioned before contribute to increase the interest of the museum collection; they play an important educational role as well. They make an attractive resting space for the tourists and the citizens of Paris who often enjoy their lunch there (there is a school nearby).

6. THE GARDEN AT VILLA SAN MICHELE ON THE CAPRI ISLAND

The garden at villa San Michele on the Capri Island is an extraordinary example. The beauty of landscape inspired the Swedish doctor, writer and art collector Axel Munthe (1857-1949) to build a house here, including the sculpture loggia (Fig. 8-9), as well as the garden contained unique flora and the vantage point.

Advantages of picturesque landscape of Gulf of Naples and Tyrrhenian Sea were exploited as the background for the plants, details and works of art i.e. an original Egyptian Sphinx integrated in the garden fence.

Munthe popularized the protection of endangered species of animals and plants, thanks to this unique specimens preserved here. He has created a protected area for the migrating birds, often killed by people, acquiring additional lands Mount Barbarossa in the neighbourhood of his house [8].One could have heard the birds sing there, but also music concerts played on violins and pianos by the owner of the villa and his friends. One of the most important guests was Victoria, the Queen of Sweden, who stayed in the villa for a longer period of time for medical reasons. Munthe has written the book entitled *The story of San Michele* (first published in 1929 and translated on 45 languages) after returning to Sweden, which has popularized this place.

Nowadays, during the holidays, there are numerous musical and artistic cultural events organised in the villa. One can also participate in painting and drawing courses, as well as in lectures and literary meetings. This place is perceived as one of the most important tourist attractions in the north-west part of the island (near Anacapri). It popularises the need to protect the environment and the local cultural values that the owner of the villa was loyal to.

Fig.8. The garden at villa San Michele on the Capri Island (photoby B. Makowska, 2015).

Fig.9. The garden at villa San Michele on the Capri Island (photoby B. Makowska, 2015).

7. CONCLUSIONS

The interaction between landscape and art influence a protection of regional identity and traditional elements of the environment. They are developing awareness of the existing values, shaping perception of space and increasing sensitivity for art. They are also considerably contributing to formation of cultural models and mechanisms (Idziak and Herman 2008: 387).

The works of art in the greenery in the urban space create an ambiance of a humanism. They have both didactic and symbolic meanings. The memory of famous people, their creativity and work is essential element which built the local community's identity. It is also a factor that contributes to the growth of tourism and, indirectly, to the economic growth of the regions (Zachariasz 2006: 27,51,127).

Gardens and parks described in the paper extract the historical and landscape values while using original and sometimes surprising ideas. They result in people's higher interest in the museum collections and towns' history. They unite the spaces of towns together; they are a place to many cultural events that integrate the community. The parks also contribute to maintaining the stability of the environment and promote ecological lifestyle.

Thanks to a creative way of presenting the work of previous and contemporary artists, the gardens became a multi-layer structure where the landscape and the heritage (works of art) co-exist harmoniously. These parks broaden the knowledge of the past; they affect the way people shape their awareness and their respect to local values.

NOTES

[1] Office de Tourisme de Honfleur (2016). *Le Jardin des Personnalités*. [online] Available at: http://www.ot-honfleur.fr/ decouvrir/en-pleine-nature/le-jardin-des-personnalites/ [Accessed 2 Jun. 2016].

[2] Velg kommune (2016). *Livsgledefestival 2014*. [online] Available at: http://dittdistrikt.no/aktiviteter/680600/ livsgledefestival-2014 [Accessed 2 Jun. 2016].

[3] Guggenheim-Venice (2016). *Patsy R. and Raymond D. Nasher Sculpture Garden*. [online] Available at: http://www. guggenheim-venice.it/inglese/collections/collection2.php?id_cat=15 [Accessed 25 May 2016].

[4] Leśnikowski, W. (2000). Muzeum of Art Primitive near the Quai Branly. Interview with Jean Nouvel. *Architectura & Biznes*, Volume 10/2000, p. 40.

[5] L`Atelier Vert – Everyting French Gardening (2016). *The vegetal walls of Patrick Blanc are French gardening fantasy at its finest. The vertical garden at the Musée du Quai Branly*. [online] Available at: http://www.frenchgardening.com/ visitez.html?pid=1140712820340395 [Accessed 23 Feb. 2006].

[6] Padberg, M. (2009). *Paris. Art and architecture*. Ożarów Mazowiecki: Ullmann–Publ. Olesiejuk, p. 271.

[7] *Musée de Cluny Visitor's Guide* (2009). Paris: Publ. Musée du Moyen Age, p. 7; Mauriè, A. and Ossart, E. (2003). *Jardin medieval: une source d`inspiration*, Paris: Édition du Chène.

[8] Capri Tourism (2016). *Villa San Michele and the Axel Munthe Museum*. [online] Available at: http://www.capritourism.com/en/article?article1_id=1786#;http://www.villasanmichele.eu/en/welcome [Accessed 2 Jun. 2016].

BIBLIOGRAPHY

Białonowska, M. (2007). Musée National du Moyen in Paris in the Context of Interest in Mediaeval Culture in France during the Second Half of the Eighteenth Century and the Nineteenth Century. *Museology*, [online] Volume 48/2007, p. 235-250. Available at: http://muzealnictworocznik.com/abstracted.php?level=4&id_ issue=871644 [Access 29 Jun. 2009]

Idziak, A., Herman, K. (2008). Between a Mine and a Landscape. Transformation through a Lanscape art. Installation, Sculpture, Performance as a Tool for Reclaiming Postindustrial Lanscape, *Dissertations of Cultural Lanscape Commission*, [online] No 10, pp. 386-394. Sosnowiec: Cultural Landscape Commission of the Polish Geographical Society, Available at: http://krajobraz.kulturowy.us.edu.pl/publikacje.artykuly/ zarzadzanie/idziak.pdf [Access 2 Jun. 2016]

Makowska, B. (2010). The gardens near museums in Paris. In: A. Mitkowska, Z. Mirek, K. Hodor, eds., *The Genius loci of the place in the garden art*. Kraków: *Technical Transactions*, Volume 5-A/2010, Cracow University of Technology, pp.179-188.

Makowska B. (2012). The Sculpture Parks in Norway. In: A. Mitkowska, K. Hodor, K. Łakomy, eds., *The gardens of memory in garden art, historic and contemporary aspects*. Krakow: *Technical Transactions*, Volume 2-A/2012, Cracow University of Technology, pp.203-208.

Zachariasz A. (2006). *Green areas as a modern town creating factor with a particular role of public parks.* Krakow: Monograph No 336, Cracow University of Technology.

POZNAN CAMPUSES – ARE THEY BIOPHILIC?

Bogusz Modrzewski[1], Anna Szkołut[2]
[1]Adam Mickiewicz University, Faculty of Geographical and Geological Sciences,
Institute of Socio-Economic Geography and Spatial Management, Department of Spatial Management;
[2]Poznan University of Technology, Faculty of Civil and Environmental Engineering, Doctoral Studies

ABSTRACT

The In search of a quality of daily work, learning and simply, living with possible comfort and stress reduction, an influence of natural landscape, especially within urban context is one of the key ingredients of today's chaotic urban environment. A theory of biophilia is partly based on landscape feature preferences (savanna hypothesis) and an scientific character of natural and designed fractal features and its impact on human biology. Chosen biophilic patterns describe the natural and eligible preferences for those specific natural physical and psychological features.
This paper's subject concerns of biophilic and landscape features and qualities of chosen Poznan academic campuses - natural and manmade landscape and cityscape: Poznan University of Technology campus Poznan University of Technology Warta, Adam Mickiewicz Universiy campus Morasko, and Poznan University of Life Sciences campus. The main research question of the study is: do campuses have intentionally designed biophilic potential and to what extent it is really utilized within daily academic routine. Multiple case study method adopted in this paper includes mixed methodology of research - in one part it is author's urban evaluation of spatial and landscape phenomena compared to biophilic qualities.

Keywords
pattern language, form language, biophilic design

1. INTRODUCTION

The world „campus", a field, was coined after Princeton University location (etymonline.com). It describes organized university or college as collection of buildings and other facilities in compositional and functional relationship. Campuses obviously function not only for academic activity and research development, but also as an important place within the city. They co-create an urban and social tissue and act like life attractor, simultaneously beeing a place of natural landscape character and feel by definition (Polish equivalent to campus is „kępa": group of trees, inland island, and popular name for village, colony or district, i.e. *Saska Kępa*). Thus, university campus is not only a collection of faculty buildings. It consists of the space itself - a living room *between* buildings, or as Jan Gehl would describe it: „life between buildings" (Gehl 2009). This broadly corresponds to the term *urban interface*: „*design of the buildings and public realm, and most particularly, the interface between them*" (Urban Design Compendium 2000: 85). It is a common, accessible area, its configuration between strictly architectural (mostly private or enclosed) and urban (mostly public and accesible) physical design. Urban interface consists of:
-    arranged and living public spaces, adjacent to the building exterior outline;
-    facade (its look, feel and permeability);
-    and interior public accessible space design (lobbies, corridors, interconnectors etc).
    Its importance lays in the fact, that it is adjustable to be redesigned and transformed into more human regenerative, living environment.

The term „life", or „livingness" in architecture, corresponds to the situation, when a certain place is vital enough, life-supporting, to be regenerative and cognitive rich, it adopts to natural human physical, mental and physiological needs, or „*to give a building as much life as possible*" (Leitner 2015: 25). Thus, adaptive design approach highlights the importance of combining functional and formal parts to: „*refer strictly to fitting the built environment to human beings, and not to abstract ideas or geometries*" (Salingaros 2008a: 223). Christopher Alexander states, that: „*function and geometry are inseparable aspects of all systems in the world*" (Leitner 2015: 22).

2. LITERATURE REVIEW

Two combined theories supports the idea of adaptive architectural and urban design: pattern language theory and biophilia theory. Theory of pattern language derives from original ideas of Christopher Alexander, in his two primary source books: *Pattern Language* (Alexander *et al* 1977) as a complete set of interconnected 253 design patterns and *The Timeless Way of Building* (1979), a broad philosophical description of pattern language theory origins and philosophy (the third book: „The Oregon Experiment", describes a pattern-generated master plan and its implementation for the University of Oregon).

A „pattern" is a scientifically justified precedent defined relation between the urban or architectural environment and its daily users experience. In its simplest definition it is a „*regularity in some dimension*" (Salingaros 2008: 130). This (regularity) can be described, systematized and transformed into real and applicable design guideline derived from and embodied in a certain system of social, health or culture values. It usually presents not a certain look, shape, or composition, but a kind of *interaction* between space traits and its users. Standard pattern takes into account (continuing) number, name (ideograph), connections with higher tier patterns, problem definition and description, state of the research, proposed solution (inc. schematic figures) and connections with lower tier patterns (Erickson 2000). Patterns may need to be apply gradually (one by one), although they are usually assembled into collections of pattern groups, or whole *pattern languages*, sets of rules enabling to „*support the development of living systems*" (Leitner 2015: 23).

The original systematization of architectural forms ale derived from numerous historical books, i.e.: *treatises, precedent book, plan book, construction manuals* and *catalogs* (Gindroz and Robins 2004). The idea of systematized design architectural concepts (albeit not allways exactly as defined as by Alexander), has ben used to describe house typological construction patterns (Mouzon 2004), house architecture (Jacobson, Silverstein and Winslow 2005), and garden design (Easton 2007). In 2013 Filelding and Nair proposed 29 patterns of school design (2013). In urban field, certain phenomena were described by Cullen (1959), a concept of place-making by Sucher (1996), and a smart growth 148 patterns in 4 categories: the region, the neighborhood, the street, and the building by Duany, Speck and Lydon (2010).

In 2008 (2008a), 2010 and 2013 Salingaros published the set of (probably simpliest possible) architectural geometric regularities, based on Alexander's opus magnum „*The Nature of Order*" (Alexander 2004), defining basic spatial organization and distribution of formal organized complexity (Modrzewski 2015c). He also defined an architectural meme („image as solution" design attitude based on ideology, trained routine or technology rather, than biological and cultural experience) and an anti-pattern, as a pattern, which triggers a couterproductive effect (Salingaros 2008a: 253, 2008b: 128). In 2015 Leitner summarized the previous original pattern theory (Leitner 2015) and Salingaros identified eight ultimate factors of biphilic design: light, color, gravity, fractals, curves, detail, water and life.

Theory of *biophilic design* assumes that certain environment content and configuration triggers significant and measurable health and cognitive effects on human physiology and psychology (including a designer himself). The term *biophilia* (love and attraction to all living beeings) coined by Erich Fromm in 1972, has been broadly popularized by Wilson, and transformed into practical, architectural and urban design contexts by Kellert, Beatley, Heerwagen, Salingaros and many others (see: Modrzewski and Szkołut 2015a). The opposite to biophilic design qualities are *biophobic*, as definied by Roger Urlich, as fear of certain animals, or David Orr, as learned, not inherited „*aversion to all living things*" (Salingaros 2015: 39) ones - not only the lack of natural features (Nature itself) but architectural structures which do not math with human perceptional capabilities, thus triggering certain health and stress consequences. Biophilic design is especially important in case of educational spaces, like campuses, as they should be perceived not only as a modern „container" for educational (academic) function, but also as a potential field of improvement and its space cognitive role.

In biophilic design context in 2002 Ole von Uexküll, Benjamin Shepherd and Corey Griffin proposed a scientific base of 246 reserch cases used by Marissa Yao (Yale School of Forestry and Environmental Studies) to create thirteen biophilic conditions (Cramer and Browning 2008: 339) and ultimately, fourteen biophilic design interconnected patterns (Browning, Ryan and Clancy 2014), in three distinctive groups:
1. Nature in the space Patterns describes presence and contact with natural, literal features and phenomena (Visual Connection with Nature, Non-Visual Connection with Nature, Non-Rhythmic Sensory Stimuli, Thermal & Airflow Variability, Presence of Water, Dynamic & Diffuse Light, Connection with Natural Systems);
2. Natural Analogues addresses natural complexity, geometry and materials used or imitated in art and architecture (Biomorphic Forms & Patterns, Material Connection with Nature, Complexity & Order);
3. Nature of the Space Patterns refers to psychological references to open and closed space configurations: Prospect, Refuge, Mystery, Risk/Peril (ibid.).

3. RESEARCH SUBJECT AND METHODOLOGY

14 biophilic design patterns theory was used to describe the space of the 3 most distinctive contemporary campuses in Poznań.

Campus Poznan Technology University *Warta* (former: *Piotrowo* or *Poligród*), was erected in 1955 (Marciniak 2010: 82), besides two other, much smaller Technology University campuses: *Wilda* and *Nieszawska* Faculty of Architecture. Location at Piotrowo (a former medieval princely village), at the right bank of the river Warta, was determined after transferring Engineering School from Wilda in 1945. Campus Warta, emerging around characteristic classicist building of Faculty of Civil and Environmental Engineering (1955, architects: S. Pogórski, L. Sternal) was designed in its conceptual form in Laboratory of Higher Education (Miastoprojekt) after 1965. Its main two most characteristic dominating modernist slab buildings (1965-1979, architects: L. Sternal, W. Milewski, Z. Skupniewicz) were the only one dominants released according to much greater, yet abandoned urban design (Książkiewicz-Bartkowiak and Kodym-Kozaczko 2013: 250). New development plans (1999 urban contest; 1st winners: M. Fikus and team, and 2008 Local Plan „Kampus Politechniki Poznańskiej w paśmie Warta" w Poznaniu), began with postmodern Lecture Center (Architecture: Studio Fikus) built till 2004, and awarded in 2005. The second characteristic new building is the futurist Faculty of Chemical Technology (2013, architects: R. Mysiak, E. Dolińska) beginning the development of the west part of the campus.

Campus Morasko, AMU (Adam Mickiewicz University in Poznań) is named after former Morasko village (and Morasko Hill), incorporated to the city of Poznań in late 80-ties of XX Century. *Campus Morasko* urban concept was released due to 1974 *Science Quarter urban contest* (Architecture and urban design contest winners: J. Gurawski, M. Fikus and J. Godlewski), although first university entirely designed campus was considered in the city downtown in early 50-ties (Marciniak, 2010: 81): on MTP Fair area, downtown districts Chwaliszewo, Śródka, north to Winiary (Marciniak 2005: 157) and according to first contest: at Marcelin (Książkiewicz-Bartkowiak and Kodym-Kozaczko 2013: 260). After 1973, the final localization was planned within Northern City Development Strip – a vast communist development linear district/city conception. After the change toward more concentric city model, the campus remained an isolated suburban island surrounded by green and open areas (Fikus, 1999: 117). The plan assumed the „L" settlement structure based on main university esplanade (Beim and Modrzewski, 2008). The following university department buildings were released since 1995 (Faculty of Physics) until present day and continuing. Thus, the Adam Mickiewicz University has actually two distinctive campuses - Morasko and inner city one (in addition to numerous other solitaire buildings). In 2003 Campus Morasko won the annual Giovanni Battista di Quadro Award.

Poznań University of Life Science, erected in 1951 main campus (except numerous other locations in the city) consists of Runge's Collegium, a neoclassical and neo-renaissance two-storey building from 1914, and (since 1968), a new modernist Collegium Maximum (1970-1978, architecture: L. Sternal, W. Milewski, Z. Skupniewicz) located near the garden neighborhood of Sołacz. The urban and arcitectural conception of the campus was developed within the Laboratory of Higher Education (Miastoprojekt) since the 60s, as a complex of buildings deliberately located in the green environment and with interesting and rich urban design program: sheltered passages, open water and characteristic sculpture of the sower. Completed buildings represent only a small part of the original urban design assumption (Książkiewicz-Bartkowiak and Kodym-Kozaczko 2013: 250).

Biophilic patterns in university campus design - proposed detailed evaluation:

P1. Visual Connection with Nature

1. Urban interface designed as functional and visual interconnection with natural landscape (5)
2. At least half of room openings directed toward natural landscape (4)
3. Visual contact from interior urban interface part to natural landscape (3)
4. At least some of the interior spaces filled with green features (2)
5. Natural landscape view not available (0)

P2. Non-Visual Connection with Nature

1. Urban interface and interior design enables sitting, learning and working in natural surroundings (5)
2. Urban interface and/or interior design enables contact with living water (4)
3. Urban interface enables contact with living plants / green walls, terraces (3)
4. Urban interface connected to natural routes (2)
5. None of above (0)

P3. Non-Rhytmic Sensory Stimuli

1. Natural sounds (5)
2. Water white noise (4)
3. Naturally changing light / shadow conditions (3)
4. Reflections / scents (2)
5. None of above (0)

P4. Thermal & Airflow Variability

1. Perforated building urban interface (5)
2. Natural ventilation systems, atriums (4)
3. Building orientation and massing (3)
4. Window control (2)
5. None of above (0)

P5. Presence of Water

1. Structures centered around significant water body (5)
2. Structures adjacent to significant water body (4)
3. Living water inside building public space interior (3)
4. Structures at the visual vicinity or walking distance to water body (2)
5. No water body in sight or walking distance (0)

P6. Dynamic & Diffuse Light

1. Most of learning and work spaces naturally lit from multiple angles (5)
2. Some of the interior rooms has acess to multiple angle light (4)
3. Interior lobbies has acess to natural light from multiple angles (3)
4. Perforated urban interface (arcades) (2)
5. least than a half rooms has acess to natural light (0)

P7. Connection with Natural Systems

1. Connection to natural habitats / systems (5)
2. Stormwater natural systems (4)
3. Heat / light / daylight gaining systems, etc. (3)
4. Design natural materials - transition (aeging) in time (2)
5. None of above (0)

P8. Biomorphic Forms & Patterns

1. Exterior/inteirior architectural cognitive-rich details (5)
2. Interior surface cognitive-rich ornament/patterns (4)
3. Proportional interior sequences/divisions (3)
4. Exterior/interior biomorphic accents (2)
5. None of above or extent overuse of aggresive forms (0)

P9. Material Connection with Nature

1. Interior content aware natural (real) materials (5)
2. Interior content aware color implementation (4)
3. Exterior natural materials (3)
4. Exterior color / or artificial material corresponding to natural (2)
5. None of above, abstract or lack (grey, black) color implementation (0)

P10. Complexity & Order

1. Fractal information-rich hierarchical structures (d=1.3 - 1.75) (5)
2. Self-similarity (at least 3 iterations) or fractal artwork in interrior design (4)
3. Fractal facades (3)
4. Fractal skyline (2)
5. Absence or extensive overuse of complicated geometry (d<1.2, d>1.8) (0)

P11. Prospect

1. Distant organized prospect (over 30 meters) connected to building urban interface (5)
2. Short interesting prospects (4)
3. Building terrace or balcony vistas (3)
4. Transparent stairwell (2)
5. None of above (0)

P12. Refuge

1. Interior and exterior system of personal learning spaces (5)
2. Interior only designed personal learning spaces (4)
3. Exterior designed personal learning spaces (3)
4. Exterior occasional / implrovised learning spaces (2)
5. None of above (0)

P13. Mystery

1. Complex designed system of *discovery* places (5)
2. Designed Obscured garden places (4)
3. Natural obscured places (3)
4. Complex curvilinear path experience (2)
5. None of above (0)

P14. Risk/Peril

1. Multistorey transparent atrums / catwalks (5)
2. Gravity challenging objects (4)
3. Transparent facades (3)
4. Challenging pedestrian transitions (2)
5. None of above (0)

4. RESULTS

4.1. Campus Poznan Technology University

Nature in the space Patterns: The campus is organized around busy car axis (ul. Berdychowo) literary splitting it into two distinctive parts: old east one and new west one (IP), seen as a whole as river Warta waterfront (OP). Physical access to the only adjacent water feature: river Warta, is blocked by the rear road and river slope although some parts of the west facade, inner lobby, library and some lecture rooms of Campus Library building are opened to the river view, according to original design (P1, P5). The significant and accessible designed green places are placed mostly around and between Faculty of Civil and Environmental Engineering building and Faculty of Machines building in the old part of the campus (P2). There are river facade benches, but (suprisingly), faced in opposite direction to the river. The second near river building - Faculty of Chemical Technology is inverted backwards to the river. Outside it there are few arranged stepped benches, but (again-suprisingly) without backs. Nevertheless, the Campus has the most freestanding benches of all the other two cases. In front of the new Library Building there is a significant yet inaccessible green circle, the most characteristic center public place in the new campus to be a place of Light and Water Spire (Fikus 2014). The only inward atriums within Faculty of Civil and Environmental Engineering building remain virtually unused as a public space (P4). Except the river Warta, there is relatively close (within five minute walk, yet problematic due to relatively dangerous pedestrian crossing via Jana Pawła II Street) access to the Lake Malta, a recreational area (P7).

Natural Analogues: There is no distinctive biomorphic forms in any scale and no purposeful cognitive use of natural materials or other systems inside or outside buildings, as well as reference to fractality in architecture, except the oldest classical facade of Faculty of Civil and Environmental Engineering building (P10). The prevalent character of architecture refers to modern, postmodern, neo-modern or futuristic style, with little attention to the most human scale and form material, ornament or detail (1mm-2m).

Nature of the Space Patterns: The basics of the original 1999 urban design plan are organized around strong awareness of the compositional, and view axes. Organized axes and prospect are intended to be faced toward the river view and three main hyper-dominants in its background (P11). The campus has no intentionally organized refuge or mystery places, although it has the access to the hidden, yet interesting Karol Kurpiński municipal park (P12). The risk / peril factor has been reached by catwalks in Library building (P14).

4.2. Campus Morasko (AMU)

Nature in the space Patterns: Although the campus is situated into open area context (IP), few of the natural surroundings parts except the window view are intentionally connected to the campus urban interface and learning rooms, as the campus buildings are designed as the autonomous buildings disconnected by vast space intervals and with facades without an element of permeability. Modern (or postmodern) facades are linked by individual car communication and parking system (OP). East part campus buildings have direct visual access to the green spaces (P1). Buildings at west part of the campus has the north entrances and main lobbies visually opened toward woods (access blocked by the impenetrable fence).

Interior urban interface in Faculty of Biology department, as the only one, is strongly filled with green features (P2). The only designed outer space (of the whole campus) to the learning purposes is a stone garden near the Faculty of Geology building. Many of the buildings has internal open air atrums (Faculties of: Geography, Geology, Social Sciences, Chemistry, History) with (little) green and (sometimes) living water, as the only sensory stimuli (P3), but designed mostly as the grey concrete air space with sitting „caskets" (P4). Sitting outside buildings on benches are not organized into larger social configurations or designed places, although use of lawns is possible. The significant larger water body is accessible via short walking distance (P5). The overal urban interface is not coherent, although some elements has the possible natural view (P7).

Natural Analogues: As in the rest of the campuses, there is no special use of biomorphic forms in various scales. Natural (ageing) materials visible only in facade elements of the sport facility (P9). Fractal, hierarchical and or self-similar architecture features are not present. The architecture is mostly postmodern or neo-modern in character, without emphasize on direct human cognitive scale.

Nature of the Space Patterns: The characteristic and larger west part of the campus, flanking the main esplanade, generates the long perspective (prospect) view to the west (P11), although most of the visual field view is filled with vast parking lots. There is no significant designed refuge or mystery features. The risk and peril elements are created by glass catwalks in Faculty of Chemistry building (P14).

4.3. Poznań University of Life Science

Nature in the space Patterns: Main campus organized at (relatively) compact lot. Although mostly modern buildings (except Runge College) has closed impenetrable urban interfaces, building configuration intentionally divides the area into several distinctive open spaces - two of them are central to public life. In north-east part vast untapped open space (IP) is definitely worth to be redesigned to more public access. The smaller south-west one (OP) is an interestingly designed, pedestrian friendly and arranged as visual (P1) and accessible open space Another very interesting part is a north-west strip of open space along Runge's Collegium and Pilot Station of Biotechnology building, with several arranged learning and resting spaces (P2). The central place is a student wooden canteen, covered walkway (P4) creating a composition axis and popular meeting and main route between main buildings. In the center of the smaller south-west area, an accessible water features creates an intimate, park like composition (P5).

Natural Analogues: Natural analogues are represented by strong natural material and structural hierarchical construction of central wooden canteen (P9, P10). A kind of a human scale accent is a monument of a peasant sower placed in front of the main building in 1979 (a copy of the original one erected in 1923 in Luboń).

Nature of the Space Patterns: Open spaces provide view interesting perspective views toward Runge's Collegium (P11). In south-west area garden wooden constructions shielding benches provide good refuge effect (P12). The overall garden design, although relatively small, contains several intriguing hidden locations (P13).

5. CONCLUSIONS

14 biophilic patterns should be treated and as a design reccomendation primarily in search of a human scale, experience and (urban interface) interaction. The three mentioned campuses pose an interesting future design field mostly in two domains - analogues to biomorphic, fractal features of natural landscape (P2), and in psychological response to urban design (P3) taking into account the possibility of the organization of a clearly regenerative spaces. Among examined places, the AMU Morasko scored the greatest biophilic potential, mostly due to its natural surroundings. The best human scale urban interface

(in its outer part) undoubtedly belongs to Poznań University of Life Science, even though its modenist origins. Best biophilic feature (yet still unused) of the Campus Poznan Technology University is its water proximity of river Warta and Malta lake.

Fig.1. 14 Design Biophilic Patterns.

Table 1. Biophilic design pattern results

Pattern	CAMPUS		
	Poznan Technology University	AMU Morasko	University of Life Science
	Pattern Score	Pattern Score	Pattern Score
P1	3	3+2	0
P2	0	2	5+4+3
P3	0	4	0
P4	0	4	3
P5	4+2	3+2	5+2
P6	4	4+3	3
P7	0	5	2
P8	0	0	0
P9	0	3	3
P10	0	0	0
P11	5+3	5+2	4
P12	2	2	3+2
P13	3	3	4
P14	5+3	5+3	3
total	34/196 (17%)	55/196 (28%)	46/196 (23%)

BIBLIOGRAPHY

Alexander, C. (1979). *The TImeless Way of Building*. New York: Oxford University Press.

Alexander, C. (2004). *The Nature of Order*. Berkeley: The Center of Environmental Structure.

Alexander, C. *et al.* (2008). *Język wzorców. Miasta, budynki, konstrukcja*. Gdańsk: Gdańskie Wydawnictwo Psychologiczne.

Beim, M. and Modrzewski, B. (2008). Dostępność transportowa i układ przestrzenno-funkcjonalny kampusu uniwersyteckiego Morasko w Poznaniu. In: Markowski, T., ed., *Rola wyższych uczelni w rozwoju społeczno-gospodarczym i przestrzennym miast*. Warszawa: Komitet Przestrzennego Zagospodarowania Kraju PAN, pp. 297-310.

Browning, W., Ryan, C. and Clancy J. (2014). *14 Patterns of Biophilic Design: Improving Health & Well-Being in the Built Environment*. Terrapin Bright Green.

Cramer, J. S. and Browning, W. D. (2008). Transforming Building Practices Through Biophilic Design. In: Kellert, S. R., Heerwagen, J.H. and Mador, M. ed., *Biophilic Design: The Theory, Science, and Practice of Bringing Buildings to Life*. Hoboken: Wiley, pp: 335-346.

English Partnership and The Housing Corporation, 2000. *Urban Design Compendium*. Llewelyn-Davies.

Erickson, T. (2000). *Lingua Frances for Design: Sacred Places and Pattern Languages*, Proceedings of Designing Interactive Systems (DIS 2000, 17-19 Aug), Brooklyn, NY: ACM Press, 2000.

Fikus, M. (1999). *Przestrzeń w zapisach architekta*. Poznań: Wydział Architektury i Planowania Przestrzennego Politechniki Poznańskiej.

Fikus, M. (2014). Architektura miejsca. Kampus Politechniki Poznańskiej Warta. In: J. Wiesiołowski et al. ed., 2014. *Kronika Miasta Poznania 2004 1: Warta*. Poznań: Wydawnictwo Miejskie Posnania, pp. 315-337.

Gehl, J. (2009). *Życie między budynkami*. Kraków: Wydawnictwo RAM.

Gindroz, R. and Robinson, R. (2004). *The Architectural Pattern Book*. New York: W. W. Norton.

Książkiewicz-Bartkowiak, D. and Kodym-Kozaczko, G., ed. (2013). *Projekt – Miasto. Wspomnienia poznańskich architektów*. Poznań: Wydawnictwo Miejskie Poznania.

Leitner, H. (2015). *Pattern theory: Introduction and Perspectives on the Tracks of Christopher Alexander*. HLS Software.

Marciniak, P. (2010). *Doświadczenia modernizmu. Architektura i urbanistyka Poznania w czasach PRL*. Poznań: Wydawnictwo Miejskie.

Modrzewski, B. and Szkołut, A. (2015a). Biofilia - teoria i praktyka projektowa. In: Górski, F. and Łaskarzewska-Średzińska, M., ed., *Biocity*. Warszawa: Fundacja Wydziału Architektury Politechniki Warszawskiej, Naukowy Klub Architektury, pp. 123-130.

Modrzewski, B. and Szkołut, A. (2015b). Architektoniczne aspekty redukcji stresu w miejscach pracy. In: M. Makara-Studzińska, ed., *Aspekty zdrowotne związane ze stylem życia*. Lublin: Uniwersytet Medyczny w Lublinie, pp. 106-119.

Modrzewski, B. and Szkołut, A. (2015c). Metoda Salingarosa w waloryzacji architektury ceglanej Poznania i okolic. In: Staszewska S., ed., *Wybrane współczesne aspekty rozwoju miast i obszarów wiejskich*. Prace z zakresu gospodarki przestrzennej. *Studia i Prace z Geografii*, nr 50. Poznań: Bogucki Wydawnictwo Naukowe, pp. 27–36.

Marciniak, P. (2005). Architektura i urbanistyka Poznania w latach 1945-1989. In: T. Jakimowicz, ed., *Architektura i urbanistyka Poznania w XX wieku*. Poznań: Wydawnictwo Miejskie, pp. 144-227.

Mouzon, S. (2004). *Traditional Construction Patterns*. New York: McGraw Hill.

Robakowska, A. and Trybuś, J., 2005. *Od zamku do browaru. O architekturze Poznania ostatnich stu lat*. Poznań: Galeria Miejska arsenał.

Salingaros, N. A. (2008a). *A Theory of Architecture*. Solingen: Umbau-Verlag.

Salingaros, N. A. (2008b). *Anti-Architecture and Deconstruction*. Solingen: Umbau-Verlag.

Salingaros, N. A. (2010). *Twelve Lectures on Architecture. Algorithmic Sustainable Design*. Solingen: Unbau-Verlag.

Salingaros, N. A. (2013). *Unified Architectural Theory: Form, Language, Complexity*. Kathmandu: Vajra Books.

Salingaros, N. A. (2015). *Biophilia & Healing Environments: Healthy Principles for Designing the Built World*. Terrapin Bright Green.

REMOTE SENSING AND GIS IN THE GEOMORPHOMETRIC ANALYSIS OF KADWA RIVER BASIN, NASHIK DISTRICT, MAHARASHTRA, INDIA

Vinayak B. Kale

Department of Geography, KKW Arts, Science and Commerce College, Pimpalgaon (B),
Tal- Niphad, Dist- Nashik, Maharashtra, India

ABSTRACT

Geomorphometric analysis of Kadwa river Basin is done through the analysis and evaluation of various drainage and topographic parameters. The analysis of various linear and areal aspects have revealed that the topographical configuration and geomorphic setting of the basin has assumed a dendritic to sub-dendritic drainage pattern with 6th order drainage. The present paper is to find out geomorphometry of Kadwa basin of Nashik District. The river Kadwa traversed for a distance of 93.14 Km. and basin covers partially two tahasils of Nashik District. With the help of Survey of India toposheets i.e. 46H/10, 46H/11, 46H/15, 46H/16, 46L/4 and satellite thematic maps like base map, drainage map, drainage density, stream frequency have been prepared using ArcGIS 10.1 software. In the basin Geometry form factor, shape factor, elongation ratio, texture ratio, drainage texture, compactness coefficient, drainage density, relief ratio has been calculated

Keywords
drainage density, form factor, shape factor, elongation ratio, texture ratio, drainage texture, compactness coefficient

1. INTRODUCTION

According to Hagget geo-morphometry is the science "which treats the geometry of the landscape" and quantitative procedure for quantifying the land surface.

2. DESCRIPTION OF THE STUDY AREA

The Kadwa river basin is extended between **20^{0}0'23.851 N to 20^{0}26'20.849 N** latitudes and **73^{0}37'24.073 E to 74^{0}11'10.05 E** longitudes (Map 1) covering an area of 16863.92 Km^2. The river originates from the Kem hill ranges at a height of 840 m and runs towards east to join the Godavari river. The river is 93.14 Km. long with major tributaries from joining from its left and right. The notable tributaries are Unanda, Parashari, Kajali and Vainatha from the left and Kolwan from the right side. The study area falls in Survey of India (1:50,000) toposheets No. 46H/10, 46H/11, 46H/15, 46H/16 and 46L/4.

Table 1. Data used and sources

Sr. No.	Data Layer/ Maps	Source
1	Topographical Map	Topographical Map, Survey of India (1:50,000)
2	Remote Sensing Data	
3	Geomorphology Map	Lanforms/geomorphological map prepared using remote sensing data, ASTER-DEM with limited field checks.
4	Morphometric Analysis	Quantitative analysis has been done based on Survey of India (SOI) toposheets and cartosat -1 DEM data
5	Slope Map	Slope map created using ASTER-DEM of 30 m spatial resolution
6	Drainage Map	Drainage network generated in GIS environment using ASTER-GDEM data

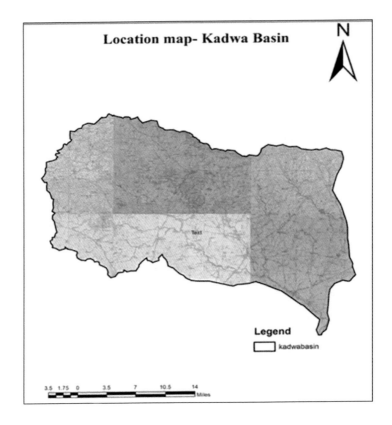

Map 1. Kadwa Basin. Location map. Prepared by author.

3. GEOMORPHOLOGY

3.1. Geo-morphometric analysis

Geo-morphometric analysis of the Kadwa river basin is carried out on the 1:50,000 scale using SOI topographic maps, Cartosat-1 DEM of 30 m spatial resolution. The stream lengths and basin areas are measured with ArcGis-10.1 software. Stream ordering is done according to the system invented by Strahler (1952) using ArcHydro tool in ArcGIS. Various methods are used for measuring linear, areal and relief aspects of the basin. Stream number, stream length, stream length ratio, bifurcation ratio, length of overland flow, form factor and stream frequency are measured according to the system proposed by Horton (1932 and 1945) Stream ordering, weighted mean bifurcation ratio, mean stream length and ruggedness number are measured using the methods proposed by Strahler (1952 and 68) Parameters such as basin area, length of the basin, elongation ratio, texture ratio and relief ratio are quantified according to Schumm. Other parameters like circulatory ratio as per Miller(1960), slope analysis as per Wentworth (1930), compactness coefficient as per Gravelius (1914), drainage texture as per Smith (1939) are quantified (Map 2).

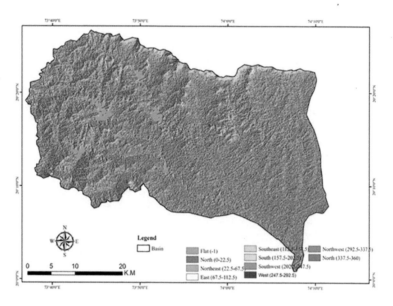

Map 2. Linear Aspects. Prepared by author.

3.2. Stream order (Su)

Stream ordering is an integral part of the quantitative analysis of any drainage basin. Horton invented stream ordering system in 1945, later on Strahler (1952) has suggested some modifications. The Stream of Kadwa basin has been ranked according to the Stream ordering system suggested by Strahler (1952). According to the system, the Kadwa River was found to be a 6th order drainage basin. (Table 2 and Figure 5) It is also seen that there is a decrease in stream frequency as the stream order increases in the Kadwa river basin.

3.3. Stream number (Nu)

Strahler's scheme of stream ordering system of the Kadwa river basin has been obtained from toposheets and CartoSAT-1 DEM. Table 2 shows the order wise stream numbers and length of streams of Kadwa river basin. Maximum frequencies are in the first order streams (3928) and minimum in the sixth order streams (1).

3.4. Stream length (Lu)

All the streams of the Kadwa river basin of various orders have been extracted from the SOI topographical sheets and updated with IRS-P5 CartoSAT-1 DEM data. Later on, order wise Lu of all streams is computed using ArcGIS version 10.1software. Hortons law of stream lengths supports the theory that geometrical similarity is preserved generally in the basin of increasing order (Strahler, 1952). Table 2 illustrates the total length of stream segments are maximum for first order streams (Fig. 6) Generally basin length decreases as the stream order increases.

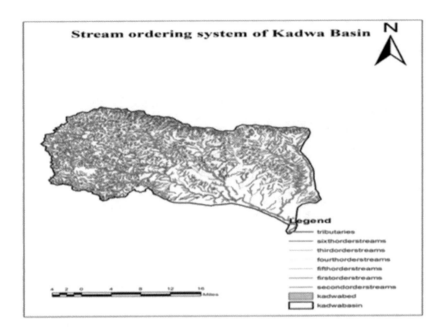

Map 3. Kadwa Basin. Stream ordering system. Prepared by author.

3.5. Bifurcation ratio (Rb)

The ratio of number of the stream segments of given order "Nu" and the number of streams in the next higher order (Nu+1) is called bifurcation ratio. Horton (1945) has find out index of relief and dissertation. The Rb is dimensionless property and generally ranges from 3 to 5. But in the Kadwa basin, it is observed that Rb is differing from one order to its next order ranging from 4 to 9 as these irregularities are determined by geological and lithological development of the drainage basin. The higher values of Rb (Table 2) in the basin indicates a strong structural control on the drainage pattern, while the lower values are indicative of basin that are not affected by structural disturbances, which seen in sixth order.

4. BASIN GEOMETRY

4.1. Form factor (Ff)

Horton (1932) has defined the Form factor as the ratio of basin area to square of the basin length (Ff=A/Lb^2). For a perfectly circular basin, the Ff value is always <0.754. If the value decreases, the basin form will be automatically elongated. Basins with the high Ff have high peak flows of shorter duration. Ff value of Kadwa basin is found to be **0.039** which indicates that the basin is compact in shape and has flow of shorter duration.

Table 2. Stream order wise total no. of streams, total length, mean length, length ratios
and Weighted mean stream length ratio.
Where: Su: Stream order, Nu: Number of streams, Lu: Stream length, Lur: Stream length ratio,
Lur-r: Stream length used in the ratio, Luwm: Weighted mean stream length ratio, Rb: Bifurcation ratio,
Rbm: Mean bifurcation ratio

Su	Nu	Lu	Rb	Lu/ Nu	Lur
I	3828	2319.13		0.61	
II	946	830.23	4.05	0.88	1.45
III	180	368.44	5.26	2.04	2.34
IV	29	112.01	6.21	3.87	1.89
V	3	11.97	9.67	3.99	1.04
VI	1	2.96	1.5	1.48	0.75
Total	4987	3644.74	26.69	12.87	7.47
Mean			5.34		1.50

4.2. Shape factor (Sf)

According to Horton (1945) the shape factor is the ratio of the square of the basin length and basin area ($Sf= Lb^2/A$) Sf is necessary proportionate to the form factor ratio (Ff). The Sf value of Kadwa basin is computed as **25.93**, indicating the compact shape of the basin.

4.3. Elongation ratio (Re)

Schumm (1956) has defined the elongation ratio as the ratio of diameter of a circle of the same area as the basin and the maximum basin length (Re) $=2/Lb* (A\pi)^{1/2}$ Strahler (1952) has classified the elongation ratio as circular (0.9 -1.0) oval (0.8 -0.9), less elongated (0.7-0.8), elongated (0.5 -0.7), and more elongated (less than 0.5). The Re of Kadwa basin is **0.6958** , which represented the basin is less elongated i.e. compact.

4.4. Texture ratio (Rt)

Texture ratio is an important factor in the drainage morphometric analysis which depending on the underlying lithology, infiltration capacity and relief aspect of the terrain (Schumm,1956). The Rt is expressed as the ratio between the first order streams and perimeter of the basin ($Rt=N_1/P$). The Rt of the Kadwa basin is computed as **18.31** and categorized as moderate in nature.

4.5. Drainage texture (Dt)

Horton (1945) has expressed the drainage texture as the total number of streams of all orders per perimeter area (Dt =Nu/P). Smith (1938) has classified drainage texture into five different textures as very coarse (<2), coarse (2-4), moderate (4-6), fine (6-8) and very fine (>8). The drainage texture value of Kadwa basin is calculated as **2.96**, which indicates a **coarse** drainage texture.

4.6. Compactness coefficient (Cc)

As per Gravelius (1914) compactness coefficient is the ratio of perimeter of basin and circumference of circular area ($Cc=0.2841*P/A^{1/2}$) The Cc is independent of size of the basin and dependent on the slope. The Cc value for Kadwa river basin is calculated as **1.44.**

5. DRAINAGE TEXTURE ANALYSIS

5.1. Stream frequency (Fs)

Horton (1932) has introduced the stream frequency as a measurable area parameter of drainage morphometry and defined it as the number of stream segments per unit area (Fs=Nu/A) Frequency of various stream order of Kadwa basin is computed and mean stream frequency value is measured as **2.96 Km/Km²**.The distribution suggests that topographically, the Kadwa river basin is in its late youth to early mature stage.

5.2. Drainage density (Dd)

Horton (1932 and 45), Strahler (1952 and 57) and Melton (1958) have defined the drainage density as the stream length per unit area (Dd=∑Lu/A). The Dd is in fact the result of the function of various parameters, such as, climate, lithology, structures and relief history and is an important quantitative parameter in geo-morphometry analysis. The Dd of Kadwa basin river basin has been computed as **2.17 Km/Km²** indicating a 'moderate' to 'high', suggesting for the presence of moderate permeable sub-soil and thick vegetative cover.

6. RELIEF CHARACTERIZATION

6.1. Relief ratio (Rh)

The total relief of the river basin is defined as the difference between the highest point of a basin and lowest point on the valley floor. The Rh is defined as the ratio between the total relief of the basin and longest dimension of the basin parallel to the main drainage line and is calculated as Rh=H/Lb. High values of Rh indicates steep slope and high relief while lower values indicate the presence of the base rocks that are exposed in the form in small ridges and mounds in the lower degree of slope. The value of Rh for Kadwa Basin is calculated as **0.11**. It is observed that areas with low to moderate relief and slope are characterized by moderate value of Rh. Low value of Rh is mainly due to the presence of high resistant base rocks and low degree of slope in the basin.

6.2. Ruggedness Number (Rn)

The product of the basin relief and drainage density is called ruggedness number (Straler 1968), and calculated as Rn= Dd* (H/1000). The ruggedness number of Kadwa river basin is **1.70**. High ruggedness value of the basin suggests that the area is high prone to soil erosion and have soft structural complexity in association with relief and drainage density.

7. SLOPE ANALYSIS

Slope is the vital feature of Geomorphometry and important in analysis of relief. Various methods are available for the determination of slope as proposed by well-known authors. Smith (1938), Miller (1960), Pity (1969), Calef and Newcomb (1953). ASTER-Digital Elevation Model (ASTER-DEM) of 30 m spatial resolution (Map 5) is used for quantitative analysis and mapping of the slope in the basin. The area represented by each slope category is mapped , measured and frequencies of each class are formed. The mean slope is calculated in the basin with a range of 489.239.The whole basin is grouped into five classes extending from0 to 20938. It is found that 90% of the basin occupy gentle slope where agriculture is prominent. While other part 10 % area lies very steep hills of Kem mountain.

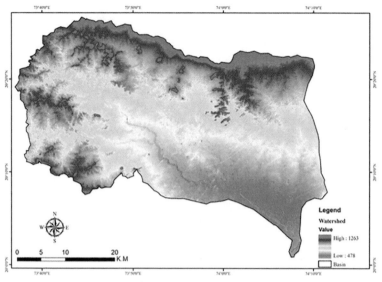

Map 4. Prepared by author.

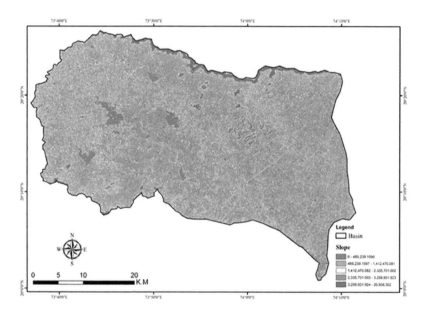

Map 5. ASTER-Digital Elevation Model (ASTER-DEM) of 30 m spatial resolution. Prepared by author.

8. RESULTS AND DISCUSSION

The study area possesses total geographical area of 209.15 km². The Geomorphometric parameters are calculated from SOI toposheets by imposing the digitized layer on it and further correction done. Most of the formulae were.

9. CONCLUSION

The Geomorphometric parameters have been derived for the entire Kadwa river basin. Kadwa river basin has sixth stream order and less elongated in shape. Drainage density of the study area is moderate to high. The stream frequency value indicates for

The geomorphometric analysis indicates that Kadwa basin possess a dendritic pattern with coarse drainage texture.

BIBLIOGRAPHY

Strahler, A. N. (1957). Quantitative Analysis of Watershed Geomorphology, Transactions, *American Geophysical Union*, Vol-38, No.6 pp. 913-920.

Umrikar, B. N., Dhanve, S. S., Dagde, G. R. and Gawai, R.O. (2013). Quantitative Geomorphological Analysis for Characterization of Selected Watersheds in Western Maharashtra, India. *International Journal of Remote Sensing and Geoscience* (IJRSG) pp. 8-15

Horton, R.E. (1932). Drainage basin characteristics, Transactions, *American Geophysical Union*, 13, pp. 350-361.

Kale, V. S. and Gupta, A. (2001). *Introduction to Geomorphology*, Orient Longman, Limited, Calcutta.

Pareta, K. and Pareta, U. (2011). Quantitative Morphometric Analysis of Watershed of Yamuna Basin, India using ASTER (DEM) Data and GIS, pp. 248-269.

Shalu, M. (2013). *Spatial Analysis of Drainage Network for Groundwater Exploration in River Basin Using GIS and Remote Sensing Techniques: A Case Study of Tons River in Allahabad*, India

National Remote Sensing Centre (NRSC): online http://www.nrsc.gov.in

Schumm, S. A. (1954). The relation of Drainage Basin Relief to Sediment Loss, *International Association of Scientific Hydrology*, 36 pp. 216-219.

Singh, S. (1992). Quantitative geomorphology of the drainage basin, Readings on remote sensing application. In: Chouhan, T. S. and Joshi, K. N. eds., Scientific publishers, Jodhpur, India. pp. 176-183

Strahler, A. N. (1964). Quantitative geomorphology of drainage basin and channel network, handbook of applied hydrology. In: *Handbook of Applied Hydrology,* Strahler, A. N. and Chow, V.T. eds., McGraw-Hill, New York, pp. 39-76

STUDY ON ARTIFICIAL WATER FEATURES IN LINE WITH DESIGN PRINCIPLES WITHIN THE CONTEXT OF SPATIAL PERCEPTION AND ENVIRONMENTAL PSYCHOLOGY: YILDIZ TECHNICAL UNIVERSITY YILDIZ CAMPUS EXAMPLE

Gülçinay Başdoğan[1], Arzu Çığ[2]

[1]Yüzüncü Yıl University Faculty of Agriculture Department of Landscape Architecture, Van/Turkey;

[2]Siirt University Faculty of Agriculture Department of Horticulture, Siirt/Turkey

ABSTRACT

Through historical process, water features in many civilizations have been effective along with satisfying different needs and actions, in increasing the quality of the places by primarily visually and secondly aurally giving a meaning in line with the symbolic values it hosts and perceptually has. Water features displaying variety in terms of functionality and aesthetics in different eras, play an important role naturally and artificially in interaction of cultural-historical-social structure and in urban identity in urban areas. Under the concept of design principles, water features trigger a psychological perception by giving meaning and movement to the place.
In this study, the reasons of use, forms, environmental impacts of artificial water features and design principles within spatial perception and environmental psychology theories have been analysed; and the comfort of the place, where it is located, and impact in utilization density in accordance with the visual, audial and psychological effects of the water features on users have been assessed within the framework of existing water features in Yıldız Technical University Yıldız Campus.

Keywords
artificial water features, environmental psychology, spatial perception, Yıldız Campus, Yıldız Technical University

1. INTRODUCTION

Water which is one the most important components of all creatures with respect to their existence and the maintenance of life, has moved beyond its vital importance as part of human life and become a form of culture and life importance of water for human beings. Besides being a basic substance, its contribution (Evyapan and Tokol 2000: 74; Cendere 1998: 2). That the first settlements were established near water underlies to the improvement of agriculture, role as a shelter and a threshold in defence, usage in transportation, and effects on the development of the social and cultural structure are substantially important. In line with all these functional characteristics, water has also symbolic values for many societies such as fertility, abundance, sanctity. Water has been acknowledged as a reflection of heaven on earth by many societies in Egypt and Mesopotamia and contact with water has been deemed to be sacred. According to some myths, water is a significant element that symbolizes the perpetuity of the universe, the rebirth and the life (Evyapan and Tokol 2000: 74; Cendere 1998: 2).

While constituting religious symbols in Old Egypt gardens, being an essential part of Ancient Greek agora's where exchange of ideas took place, serving as security channels that encircle chateaus for defensive purposes in Medieval Ages and constituting a style of Renaissance and Baroque, water elements play also a crucial part in Traditional Turkish Culture. The most important architectural structures of the Seljuk, Principalities and Ottoman periods are accompanied with water; and are related to water through fountain structures on front sides, pools in yards and şadırvans (fountains used for ritual ablutions in mosques). Water structures which functionally serve for practices like ritual ablution, cleaning and providing potable water especially in Islamic societies, have remained as monuments with social and cultural values since water has spiritually emblematized the maintenance of life (Aytöre 1962: 1-9; Cendere 1998: 2, 69).

The most important water structures of the traditional culture have generally geometrical shapes and thus bear influences of Medieval and early Renaissance water structures. The water in the square or rectangular shape water elements is preferred to be flowing, so the pools are set in motion with fountains and waterfalls (Eldem 1970: 292).

Fountains, şadırvans, formal pools with sharp edges, which were at the forefront in Turkish culture throughout history, have later been replaced by rather curled, ornamental, circular and non-formal pools and waterfalls. Especially in the 18th and 19th centuries, English gardening and landscaping movements containing curved free forms have had their impacts in Turkish culture (Zorlu 1992: 80; Eldem 1970: 292-293).

As well as fulfilling various needs and practices for many cultures in historical process, water structures have been significant elements that give particularly visual meanings to spaces where they are located in line with their symbolical value (Rees and May 2002: 7). In this context, why and in which form water elements are used, their environmental effects and design principles are examined in the light of spatial perception and theories of environmental psychology; and in accordance with the visual, aural and psychological effects of water structures on users, their impacts in terms of comfort of the space and intense use are assessed as part of water elements available at Yıldız Technical University.

2. CONTENTS

2.1. The location and the historical development of YTU campus

Beşiktaş Hill where Yıldız Palace is located and which is mentioned in Byzantine sources, praised in early Byzantine poems as 'Daphne' and described as fields in which the pretty Pan is imagined to play his flute in Daphne forests, and which has later been a valuable area belonging to the treasury during the Ottoman rule, has first attracted the attention of Suleiman the Magnificent with its very beautiful landscape and this area registered in 'the treasury of the Ottoman Sultan' (Hazine-i Hassa) was called 'Koru-u Hümayun' (the grove of the sultan). This private estate field with the name of 'Kazancıoğlu Garden' at the beginning of the 1600s was added to the sultan's property. Selim III was also amazed of the beauty of this place and commissioned a pavilion for his mother Mihrişah Sultan. And during the period of Sultan Mahmud II, the grove has gained importance as a military training field and Mahmud II commissioned a kiosk for his dearest 'Yıldız'. Abdülmecid commissioned a new kiosk named 'Kars-ı Dil Kuşa' for his mother Bezm-i Alem Sultan in 1842 and the other kiosks were demolished in the meantime. Abdulhamid II who ascended the throne on May 1876 refrained from residing in Dolmabahçe Palace and by considering that the Palace was besieged from the sea during the dethronement of Abdulaziz, he felt disturbed of the fact that this palace is vulnerable to be sieged every moment from the sea and land so he went to Yıldız Palace on April 1976 and after he moved there, the place was named "Yıldız Saray-ı Hümayunu". Besides wooden pavilions and kiosks, the last palace of the Ottomans is Yıldız Palace. In Yıldız where the kiosks of the former sultans were located, Abdulhamid II had commissioned a garden and a housing complex covering about a 500,000 m² area in a gorgeous grove, at the hills facing Beşiktaş and some gardens with beautiful scenery, viewing the entire Istanbul and Bosphorus. In sum, the extravagance of every sultan to get their own palace as traditionalized in the 19th century continued in the period of Abdulhamid II by building Yıldız

Palace. During his thirty three years of reign, Abdulhamid II encircled Yıldız with many military posts and with high and thick walls in order to ensure security, as well as adding divisions to the Yıldız pavilions in the middle of large gardens and parks to harbour crowded Harem cohorts and the Imperial Staff. In the meantime, Hasbahçe and the grove was extended to the hillsides of Ortaköy and this place shortly became a small city and the palace has been used as the administration centre of the Ottoman Empire for 44 years from 1877 to 1922 (Mutlu 2006). The area given to the Yıldız Technical School after its establishment in 1937 is today used as the Rectorate Building of Yıldız Technical University. In addition, the Çukur Saray (Hollow Palace, also named Hanım Sultanlar Dairesi, Chamber of Sultan's Wives), Bekar Sultanlar and Şehzade Köşkleri (the kiosks of Single Sultans and Princes), Sünnet Köşkü (Circumcision Kiosk), Damatlar Dairesi (Chamber of Grooms), Agavat, Kiler-i Hümayun (the Sultan's Cellar) are also utilized by the university (Anonymous 2010).

2.2. Examining the existing water elements of Yıldız Technical University in the context of spatial perception and environmental psychology

2.2.1. Water Elements Available in the Campus Area

Yıldız Technical University has water elements with different figural forms and functions at Yıldız campus (Fig.1-2).The area has 1 rectangular pool, 1 circular pool, 1 octagonal pool, 1 cascade pool and 12 fountains. However, the octagonal pool and circular pool are not used and only 2 of the fountains are in use. The location, usage and shape of the water elements in the area have been examined within the context of spatial perception and environmental ecology.

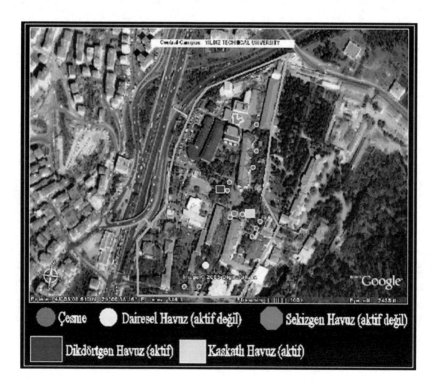

Fig.1. The Location of the Existing Water Elements in Yıldız Campus (developed from Google Earth).

The Cascade Pool

The Circular Pool in front of the Building of Civilization

The Octagonal Pool in front of the Institution of Science

The Rectangular Pool in the Middle Garden

Fountain (Active)

Fountain (Not Active)

Fig.2. The Existing Water Elements in Yıldız Campus (photographs by author).

2.2.2. The location and importance of water element at the campus area

Water can affect the human-environment relation by adding sound and texture to the space it is located in. Spaces containing water are psychologically lively, dynamic, comfortable and attractive from the viewpoint of the user and thus have the characteristic of a centre of attention (Rees and May 2002: 7). The contribution of water to open spaces in the context of human-environment relations is ranged as follows:
- Forming scenery,
- Being the focal point and directing pedestrian moves,
- Providing a different perception of the space it is located in through its reflective feature,
- Creating a cultural symbol (by the fact that water cities are important factors of identity with their images, elements of prestige, means of propaganda, and by propagating a certain feeling or thought widely and drawing attention),
- Being a religious symbol (purgation, simplicity, purity),
- Emotional and psychological effects (tranquilizing, calming, thrilling effects, expanding the imagination, being a source inspiration and audio-visual effects) (Moore 1995: 27).

The effects of the water elements existing in the campus on open space area are given in Table 1 by taking into consideration the above mentioned features.

Table 1. The Effects of the Water Elements on Open Space in Yıldız Campus (by author)

	Focal point/directing pedestrian moves	Cultural symbol	Emotional and psychological effect
The Middle Garden Rectangular Pool	x		x
The Cascade Pool	x	x	x
The Circular Pool	x		
The Octagonal Pool	x		
Fountain	x	x	

Accordingly, the middle garden rectangular pool, the cascade pool, the circular pool, the octagonal pool and fountains contribute to open space as focal point/directing pedestrian moves; the cascade pool and fountains as cultural symbols; and the rectangular pool and cascade pool as emotional and psychological effect. Considering water elements with respect to their locations; fountains are concentrated at the area of the kiosks, the rectangular pool is located at the part of cafés whereas the cascade pool lies between the routes to the buildings of and Institute of Science.

2.2.3 The use of water elements in the campus area and its reasons

As a design element, water adds action and meaning to plain surfaces and simple spaces by means of its visual quality, reflective feature and acoustic effects (Halprin 1964: 142). The characteristic aspect of water in space directly affects the character of the space and human activities. Water in open spaces can exist by springing from a point source, flowing on a linear surface, concentrating in a closed form or as a border element (Table 2) (Şengül 1995: 57). Hence the cascade pool and rectangular pool of the area are the water elements that provide the activities of assembly-watch-rest.

Taking into consideration that water transforms the space where it is located into a totally different character by giving meaning, it meets aesthetic and functional requirements in terms of water elements, space quality and user activities in open spaces (Harris and Dines 1988: 530-2; Booth 1989: 259).

As part of aesthetic reasons, water elements are basically perceived as a "visual element" in spaces. But due to the fact that people psychologically adopt water as the origin of life and the maintenance of life, they are directed towards water psychologically rather than visually. The sense of being close to and being in contact with water are interpreted as people's emotional reactions to water around them (Harris and Dines 1988: 530-2). Principally in line with the psychological perception between water elements used in open spaces and the user, visual, aural, touching effect and other perceptions play a role. In functional context, water elements fulfil aesthetic needs as well as serving functionally too many purposes. Being a focal point in space and having a directive effect are functional characteristics as much as psychological. Nevertheless the functional uses of water elements in principle range from balancing climatic comfort, controlling circulation and motions in space to obstructing noise and recreational usages (Booth 1989: 259-261; Zülfikar and Yoshikawa 2008: 237). In this context, the water elements in the campus area have been assessed in Table 3 in terms of aesthetic and functional requirements. In accordance, it serves aesthetically as visual-psychological-aural-contact touching effects and functionally as comfort-directing-recreation functions.

Table 2. The change of space identity according to the character of water (developed from Şengül 1995)

CHARACTER	ACTION	HUMAN ACTIVITY AND PERCEPTION EFFECT	EXAMPLE
Point	Water being spread from a point	Assemble and watch	Fountain (in cascade pool)
Pool	Surrounding-concentrating of water	Assemble, watch, rest and spend time	Rectangular-cascade pool
Edge	Border-brink	Assemble, watch, rest and spend time	Rectangular pool

Table 3. Aesthetic and Functional Effects of Water Elements in the Campus Area (by author)

Water Elements	Aesthetic Effect	Functional Effect
Rectangular Pool	Visual-psychological-contact touching effect	Climatic comfort-directive-recreational function
Cascade Pool	Visual-psychological-aural-contact touching effect	Climatic comfort-noise control-recreational function
Fountain	Visual-contact touching effect	Climatic comfort-directive function

2.2.4 Forms of using water element at the campus area

Water elements in the campus area are discussed in two main usage forms as static and dynamic in relation to the aesthetic values of the users and physical specifications of the space. Accordingly, the rectangular pool is examined as a static water element and the cascade pool is examined as a dynamic water element.

The Rectangular Pool: As a static water element, it contains aesthetic value as well as being used functionally due to its climatic comfort (creating microclimate) features. It has an unnatural appearance because of having sharp and smooth edges. It is clearly perceived and shows a focal feature in a space where elements with firm ground and bordering characteristics are apparent (Fig.3).

The rectangular pool and its circle are rather a transition space from the viewpoint of users. Because of being a place without sitting items around and with its steady transition circulation, users utilize the space for waiting in very limited time and for resting. The lotuses in the pool are effective on visual perception while the noises of the frogs in the water are effective on aural perception.

Cascade Pool: With dynamic water elements, it visually, aurally and psychologically appeals to all senses and affects spatial perception with its dynamism brought by motion. It strengthens the visual, aural and psychological perception by creating a dominant character in space. Various visual and aural effects occur while water hits various barriers pouring from one point to another and falling gradually. The cascade water pool which constitutes a particularly visual and aural focus in space also fulfils a task of balancing the microclimate by virtue of sprinkling water drops. Taking into consideration the environmental effects of the cascade pool, it is visually good; medium on the basis of sound level and splashing; very good in wind stability; and gives a feeling of dynamism as perceptual effect (Table 4). In addition, the fountain in the pool is distinguished artistically and aesthetically as well as symbolizing liveliness and freshness. It has a cooling effect by virtue of the irregular and free sprinkling of the drops on surfaces and contributes to balancing the microclimate.

From the users' point of view, the cascade pool and its circle are perceived as isolated from the campus area. It has very few sitting items around and is used as a space for resting, relaxing, spending time for a while and chatting in groups of two or three people. It is perceived as a space in nature with its distance to

Fig.3. The Rectangular Pool in the Middle Garden (photographs by author).

Table 4. Environmental Effect of the Cascade Pool (developed from the table in Harris and Dines, 1998: 530-6)

	FEATURES	VISUALITY	SOUND LEVEL	SPLASHING	WIND STABILITY	PERCEPTUAL EFFECT
Cascading Pools	Irregular cascading flow - medium high flow rate	Good	Medium	Medium	Very Good	Dynamism

noise, with intense sound of water and composition of plants. Pedestrian circulation is not dense due to its location. Sounds of birds and squirrels can also be heard as the area is surrounded by trees (Fig.4).

Fountains: Fountains are water elements formed by water which is poured from cisterns or springs to a reservoir by a tap through pipes or canals (Kavaklı 1994: 127). There are 12 fountains in the campus area. While some of them are located independent from elements bordering the space, others are located among, embedded in or leaning to bordering elements (buildings around, walls etc.). Two fountains are actively in use. Functionally, they were a source of drinking water in the past and presently they create a cleaning and cooling effect; constituting a focal point in the campus area (Figure 5).

Fig.4. Users at the Cascade Pool (photographs by author).

Fig.5. The Fountain Located Between Bordering Elements in the Campus Area (by author).

2.2.5. The effects of the water elements on the campus area in respect to forms of use

The relation between campus area and the water is principally put under 2 headings and varies in subheadings depending on forms of use.

The Use of Water in the Campus Area as a Highlighting Element: Highlights are created by using water in space singly or as integrated with another element depending on a specific form and size (Şengül 1995: 73). The water taps, pools and fountains are the most prominent examples in the area. Besides visual, aural and psychological effects, their functional features such as controlling circulation, balancing climatic comfort are prioritized.

The Use of Water in the Campus Area for Surrounding/Bordering: The rectangular pool in the middle garden surrounds the ground and creates a border with its firm ground and plant texture.

2.2.5.1. The effects of static water elements on the campus area

As being one of the elements being used in open urban spaces, static water elements are effective in context of 4 main functions. These create the effects of mirror, window, texture and refreshing (Erdal 2003: 59).

Functionally, the rectangular pool used in the campus area creates a texture effect. The texture effect is generated through the dark-coloured pool, dynamic water and wavelike surface.

In this context of the rectangular pool; depending on the qualities of the water elements, visual and aural properties, texture of the water surface and environmental factors, the environmental effects are as follows: good visuality, low sound level, very good wind stability and showing a focal feature in terms of perceptive effect (Table 5).

Table 5. Comparison of the Rectangular Pool with regards to Environmental Effects
(developed from the table in Erdal, 2003: 63)

	Water Level	Visuality	Sound Level	Wind Stability	Perceptive Effect/Function
Texture Effect	Wavelike	Good	Low	Very Good	Being Focal Element/ Discernible

2.2.5.2. The effects of dynamic water elements on the campus area

The effects of dynamic water elements vary principally depending on the water flow rate, intensity, water level and the distance where the water is transmitted. The effects depending on these qualities of the dynamic water elements are also related to the location, climate and surrounding properties of the space. In this context, dynamic water elements are analysed under seven topics in open spaces. These are refreshing/cooling effect, use of space as a means of play and entertainment, prestige/vanity effect, oasis effect, monumental meaning effect, metaphor effect and use of a medium of message (Symmes 1998).

The cascade pond affects the campus area in four main ways based on the water flow rate, intensity, water level and the distance where the water is transmitted (Table 6). Hence it creates the senses of relaxing, excitement and dynamism in terms of perceptive effect.

Refreshing/Cooling Effect: Creates a balancing effect on climatic comfort and a cooling effect through water drops. Balances the microclimate of the space and ensure the users to feel comfortable in the space.

Play and entertainment: With its dynamism and enthusiasm, it is interesting and exciting for users. It arouses the desire of users to touch due to its intriguing appearance and motion.

Prestige/vanity effect: It provides the affection and direction of the user in space.

Oasis effect: It provides an oasis effect at the campus because of its visual, aural and cooling features.

Table 6. Comparison of the Cascade Pool with regards to Environmental Effects
(generated from the sections in Erdal, 2003: 78-89)

	Visuality	Sound Level	Water Flow Rate	Wind Stability	Perceptive Effect/Function
Refreshing/Cooling Effect	Good	Medium	Medium/High	Good	Climatic Comfort/Relaxing-Relief
Means of Play and Entertainment	Good	High	Medium/ High	Very Good	Excitement-Dynamism-Play
Prestige/Vanity Effect	Very Good	High	High	Very Good	Magnificence-Admiration-Dynamism-Impression
Oasis Effect	Good	Medium/ High	Medium/ High	Good	Relaxing-Breathing-Having a Break

2.2.6. Vegetation of Water Elements

As the most effective design elements to enhance the attraction of water elements and as the easiest to implement and care, plants ensure natural cleaning of water and maintain other living ecosystems in terms of contributing ecological cycles. However, the principal aim in vegetation design is to compose harmony or contrast out of plants with various sizes and shapes, ensure selective perception and enrich the conditions of reflection. Appearances which refer to natural life are created in urban spaces through implementations. The plants arranged along the line where water and soil conjoin provide more natural appearances by smoothing the transition, particularly in pools with free shape (Beazley 1993: 342).

Different compositions of plants have been implemented in and around the rectangular pool in the campus area. The lotuses in the pool grow by getting plentiful sunlight and cover the pool in the spring. They also draw attention with their white flowers. The plants that are used as borders around the pool create a tight green texture in the area and border the transition spaces (Fig. 6).

The vegetation around the cascade pool creates rather a visual effect and ensures the pool to be perceived as a natural structure. The pool is completely surrounded with plant texture and is isolated from the campus area (Fig. 7).

3. CONCLUSIONS

In open spaces available for common use and which are centres of sociocultural interaction, the artificial use of water attracts people and becomes an important means in ensuring socialization. In this context, the water elements implemented in the campus area affects the human-environment relationship formally and functionally.

The rectangular pool offers the user a short-time rest, cooling because of being in the shade and contact with nature both visually and aurally, as well as constituting a focal point. Nevertheless, the space

Fig.6. Plant Composition at the Rectangular Pool (photographs by author).

Fig.7. Plant Composition at the Cascade Pool (by author).

cannot be fully perceived due to the lack of sitting items around and intense user traffic as a place of transition. The cascade pool doesn't have sufficient sitting items and doesn't allow intense use due to its location, thus the area is isolated from the campus and this has added a sense of secrecy to the space.

The fountains in the campus area represent the Ottoman period and are concentrated around the kiosks. In addition to being a marking item, it serves the functions of cooling and cleaning.

BIBLIOGRAPHY

Anonymous, (2010). www.ytu.edu.tr (acces: 01.05.2010)
Aytöre, A. (1962). Türklerde Su Mimarisi. In: *Milletlerarası 1.Türk Sanatları Kongresi*, Ankara.
Beazley, M. (1993). *The garden source book.* London: Reed International Books Ltd.
Booth, N.K. (1989). *Basic elements of landscape architectural design.* Long Grove Illinois: Waveland Pres Inc.

Cendere, A. (1998). *Su Elemanlarının Kentsel Mekanlarda ve Yeşil Alanlarda Kullanımı*. Msc. Istanbul Technical University.

Eldem, S.H. (1970).*Türk bahçeleri*. Ankara: Kültür Bakanlığı Türk Sanat Eserleri: 1, Apa Basımevi.

Erdal, Z. (2003). *Su Elemanlarının Kentsel Mekanlarda Kullanımı*, Msc. Istanbul Technical University.

Evyapan, G.A. VE Tokol, A.S. (2000). *Peyzaj tasarımı ders notları*. Ankara: METU.

Halprin, L. (1964). *Cities*. New York: Van Nostrand Reinhold Company.

Harris, C.W. and Dines, N.T. (1988). *Time saver standarts for landscape architecture*. USA: McGraw-Hill Publishing Company.

Kavaklı, K. (1994). *Su Elemanlarının Kullanımı ve İstanbul Çevre Düzenlemelerindeki Su Elemanlarının Araştırılması*. Msc. Istanbul Technical University.

Moore, C.W. (1995). "The potential of water", architectural design, architecture and water. *Profile*, 113, Vol.65, 1/2.

Mutlu, F. (2006). *XIX Yüzyıl Osmanlı Saray Bahçelerinde Batılılaşma'nın Tasarıma Etkilerinin Peyzaj Tasarım İlkeleri Açısından İrdelenmesi*. Msc. Beykent University.

Rees, Y. and May, P. (2002). *Su bahçeleri tasarım kitabı*. İstanbul: YEM Yayınları.

Symmes, M. (1998). *Fountains splash and spectacle, water and design from the renaissance to the present*. New York: Rizzoli International Publications Inc.

Şengül, E. (1995). *Mimari-Su İlişkisi Üzerine Bir İnceleme*. Msc. Istanbul Technical University.

Zorlu, D. (1992). *Tarihsel Süreç İçerisinde Su Öğesinin Peyzaj Planlamada Kullanımı*. Msc. Yıldız Technical University.

Zülfikar, C. and Yoshikawa, K. (2008). Water as a Design Element in Urban Open Spaces With Examples From Japan. In: *4. Uluslararası Mimar Sinan Sempozyumu Su ve Mimarlık*. İstanbul: 237-242.

BUILDING MODERNIZATION IN REPUBLICAN ERA. URBAN PLANNING IN TURKEY: EXAMPLE OF ANKARA AND İSTANBUL

Gülçinay Başdoğan

Yüzüncü Yıl University Faculty of Agriculture Department of Landscape Architecture, Van/Turkey

ABSTRACT

Arise of the republican regime, creating a new nation state in Turkey, led the modernization project to start to be implemented directly by the state within the borders of the country. Modernizing policy of the republic comprised transport and landscape works in large scale planning on the improvement of rural areas; and state centred modernist urban planning implementation in urban scale. Modernization project, which aimed to be operated efficiently within this framework, was implemented with creation and transformation of public areas and urban open spaces within the scope of urban planning. A new urban image tried to be established with Kemalist ideas based on the belief that the urban areas play an important role in creation of a new state order.

Within this context, this study aims to establish the understanding of planning of the era through assessing the Ankara Lorcher-Jansen Plan and Güven Park-Güven Monument from Ankara and Istanbul Prost Plan from Istanbul, among the urban planning examples with an efficient role in Republican Era, within the framework of the conducted modernization projects.

Keywords

Ankara, İstanbul, modernization, Republican Era of Turkey, urban planning

1. INTRODUCTION

The modern architecture of the Republican period can certainly not be thought independent from a process that generates urban spaces and urban planning activity. Organizing cities of a country in accordance with urbanism principles and situating place set-up to promote the new life style and forms of socialization of the modern urban society was an important target of the Republic's project of modernity. It can be said that the idea of creating a contemporary city image was determinant in pre-1950s urbanism activity (Bilsel 2009: 12).

While the urban space was gaining a new contemporary appearance with new buildings and streets in the Republican period, social life was rapidly modernizing through spaces where individuals of the modern society could gather. In the second half of the 1930s, the creating of new public spaces, such as stations/railways, parks, community centre buildings which are the urban facilities of the Republican period, entailed by the modern public life has been indicative of urban and social modernization (Tanyeli 1998: 64-67).

One substantial sign of the renewal and transformation of the Republican cities has been the building of housing estates (Bilgin 1998: 255-272). On the one hand, new spaces of social life in the cities were projected in this period and on the other hand, new dwellings in which nuclear families can live and a new culture of dwelling that completely changed the culture of life and housing up to that time emerged (Birol 2004).

With the modernization movement which developed in Turkey and constituted when Ankara became the capital city after the proclamation of the Republic, many very valuable and distinctive legal-administrative regulations, that still maintain their importance today, were made to recreate the capital city space in a planned way between 1923 and 1933. An important urban planning (The Lorcher Plan-Jansen Plan) came to the forefront with the declaration of Ankara as the capital and this city became the first Anatolian city where the modernization project was implemented following the Republic (Akın et al. 2007: 250-267).

In this period, industrialization has come to prominence by favor of the single-party state with the establishment of the Republic, the capital city İstanbul was replaced by Ankara, the "country was woven with nets of iron", small Anatolian cities on the railway routes were chosen as the locations of factories to be built as envisaged in the industrial plans which started to be implemented as a result of the statist policy developing after 1929 (Bilgin 1998: 255-272). In the first years of the Republican Turkey, a conceptual structure is witnessed in which the "Healthy City" and "Beautiful City" approaches remained but gradually started to give way to the "Practical City" movement (Dinçer and Akın 1994: 127-131).

The phenomenon of planning spreading from Ankara was influential on the regulation of urban development between the years of 1930 and 1950. In many cities, a dual centre consisting of newly developed administrative functions with services oriented to these and a traditional centre coalesced with the old city texture was distinctively seen (Akın et al. 2007: 250-267). The Republican administration changed the legislation remained from the Ottomans with the laws enacted between 1930 and 1935 and made new institutional arrangements (Municipal Law, Public Sanitation Act, Municipal Bank Law of Establishment, 1/500 Scale Implementation Plans, Municipality Road and Buildings Code etc.).

Following the Republican period, the system attempted to be developed in the institutional structure in the 1930s has moved the urban management and urban planning approach of that time to the 1980s and even beyond (H. Jansen's Plan, Municipal Acquisition Act, General Regulations of Urban Development Plan Arrangement, Provincial Bank, the Law on Municipal Revenues, etc.) (Dinçer and Akın 1994: 127-131).

2. CONTENTS

2.1. The modernization process in Turkey

The modernization movement which manifested itself as social and intellectual transformations in the 17th century and later took effect across the world has a multi-layered structure. By philosophically having an enlightened, rationalist and planning-oriented essence, institutionally having a nation-state based democratic structure, economically having mass production and consumptions patterns and socially having a vision of the citizen with property right; modernity denotes a process formed by all these layers (Olgun 2003: 14-23).

The urbanization experience in the Republican period was formed through the principles of independence and national development. These principles must be thought in two different levels. One of them is to transform territorial space to a nation-state space and the other is to arrange the cities as places of modernity (Tekeli 2009: 111). In accordance with these principles, spatial strategy at the macro scale consists of three layers. The first of them contains selecting and developing the capital city, the second contains balanced regional development and finally the third contains to link together the dispersed Anatolian settlements for total control of the national market and country spaces.

The capital Ankara which is chosen in the middle of Anatolia reflects the spatial logic of the new nation-state. For the Kemalist regime, such a choice is also the expression of national unity, centralization and creating a homogenous social structure around a particular identity (Tankut 1990; Tekeli 1984). The most important factor for the city to gain a size and versatility to that allows its own growth is that it possesses decision making functions and despite the efforts in the development of the city are not made in a planned fashion, it contains versatility. Administrative functions being gathered in the city provided the city to develop (Tekeli 2008: 54).

The balanced regional development policy is a historic breaking point for Anatolia. Anatolian cities with under a population of ten thousand have been chosen for industrial investments determined through statist policies that became evident in the 1930s; the urban development in these cities has later been supported with public services and transportation investments. The factories here were established to fulfill some other targets as well as to make a particular production. One of these targets was that these points would bring social change to its environment and the other was to provide these places to develop by its own by enabling the private sector to flourish where it is established (Tekeli 2008: 52). Small cities like Nazilli, Kırıkkale and Eregli where SOEs (State-Owned Enterprises) was established have been the fastest-growing cities of the Republican period. While the annual average growth rate of these cities was 5% in the first decade, the population growth of the big cities such as Izmir and Istanbul has been about 1.4%. As a result of regional development policies, the nationwide geographical distribution of the population in this period has become more balanced compared to the previous one (Şengül 2009: 115).

Rather than ensuring the integrity of the domestic market, the railway system under the Ottomans developed towards the integration of different regions of the country with the economy of the external powers whose influence they were under. There were disconnected lines in the system because it was developed by foreign companies that didn't want to cooperate with each other. An Ankara based railway network created in the Republican period by opening new lines on one hand and nationalizing the lines of foreign companies on the other (Tekeli 2009: 156-157). The railways are not constructed in accordance with a specific program. The presence of a particular principle can be seen despite it was not planned. A network is established among the installed lines and this network is linked to port cities. Another characteristic is to cover the whole country with railways. It seems that the highway system in this period merely developed as a network which feeds the railways (Tekeli 2008: 55). Extending the transportation network to the end points was crystallized as a spatial policy which was given importance in terms of national integrity and gaining control.

2.1.1. Planning works at the national level

Planning works at the national level was directly conducted by the state through the modernity project within national boundaries with the Republic regime which led to a new nation-state to be born. A new state order emerged in many areas with the modernity project that was aimed to be managed efficiently. In this context, many policies were developed especially in the early Republican period (1923-50). These policies have contained the industry, transportation, agriculture and the institutions and laws as part of planning and protection.

2.1.1.1. Industrial policies

The new regime being established in Ankara made several political and legal regulations to accelerate the industrialization of Turkey. After the proclamation of the Republic, the 1913 Law on the Encouragement of Industry was retained in force until a new one is enacted. Also the Turkish Bank of Industry and Mining established in 1925 began to give credits to private industrial enterprises and buy their stock certificates to help them to form their capital (Keyder 1978: 210-250). In addition, granting a production monopoly and several prerogatives to a company that wants to establish sugar mills in Turkey in 1925 indicated clearly the support of the government to private capital in the industry. Until 1927, the number of enterprises benefited from the 1913 Law for the Encouragement of Industry increased to 239 in 1913, to 342 in 1923 and to 470 in 1927. One of the most important breakthroughs of the industry and investment policy in the period of 1923-1929 was the enactment of the Law on the Encouragement of Industry numbered 1055 and dated 28 May, 1927. Many facilities were provided to the manufacturing and mining industries with this law which was accepted to remain in force for 15 years. The statist policy in the 1930s has led to positive outcomes for capital accumulation in general (Tezel 1994). The establishment of the Central Bank was a crucial moment in the economic program prepared by the government in 1930 (Çelebican 1982: 23-24). With the Industry Office and Industrial Loan Bank established in 1932, the customs exemptions in the importation of raw materials were removed; the Industry Office and Industrial Loan Bank was replaced by the establishment of Sümerbank in 1933 due to the problems occurred in the approach of the government to the industrial policy; customs exemptions in the importation of raw materials and machines were implemented again in June, 1933 (Tekeli and İlkin 1982). As a result of the failure of the policy focused on the private sector with the effects of the Great Depression of 1929, a series of laws were enacted between 1930-1933 to regulate import and control export. In the need to make a planned industry, the first five-year industrial plan was prepared (Ezer 2005).

The first Five-Year Industrial Plan was prepared in 1933 and the second Five-Year Industrial Plan, which was going to enter into force in 1938, was prepared in 1936. The main rationale of the First Five-Year Industrial Plan can be summarized briefly as following: to create an independent nation of Turkey means to turn Turkey into an economically independent and fully fledged unity. The measures required in this sense are regarded as a whole comprising agriculture and industry. "Import substitution" which has become a tradition of the Turkish industrialization policy and increasing the production of imported consumer goods in Turkey were started by the state and systematically with this plan (DPT 2010). The key feature of the five-year plan was that it included the industry whose raw materials were available or could be supplied in Turkey. The main industries that exceed the economic power of the private sector would be established by the state so new fields of activities would be created for the private sector with cheap and easily accessible semi-finished goods (İnan 1972). These principles were also determined in accordance with the "Economic National Pact" adopted in the first Turkish Economic Congress organized in Izmir in 1923 (DPT 2010).

The five-year plan contains five groups of main industries. These are: textile industry, mining industry, cellulose (raw material of paper, cardboard etc.) industry, ceramic industry and chemical industry. The industry branches to be established within the scope of the plan were elaborated in details at the commissions, suggestions were made to select the locations of the facilities to be built and the Cellulose and Paper Industry facilities was predicted to be established in Izmir. The prominent factors in selecting the locations were: the abundance and cheapness of transport vehicles, the forests where the trees would be provided from not being distant, the availability of the great need of water and the recruitment of labour power (İnan 1972). It is seen that Istanbul, Izmir and the shorelines were avoided by considering the suggestions of the General Staff about choosing location and as a result, the iron-steel and chemical facilities were located in Karabük (Tekeli and İlkin 1982).

The goals of the Second Five-Year Industrial Plan whose principals were determined at the Industry Congress convened in Ankara on 20-24 January, 1936 and which was planned to put into force in 1938 were considered broader compared to the First Plan. Its analysis's was made more extensively and the priorities focused on investment goods and intermediate goods. This Plan which comprised the previously prepared "Mines Plan" couldn't be put into force due to the changing conditions of the internal and external effects of the Second World War, but a certain part of circa 100 factories planned to be established was able to be materialized in the following years (DPT 2010). The Second Industrial Plan aims at improving the industry together with the development of the agricultural sector in Turkey where the essential structure is agricultural.

2.1.1.2. Transportation Policy

In the transportation policy, predominantly railways are given importance. The railway lines were nation-alized in 1924 and "General Directorate of Anatolia-Baghdad Railways" was established. It was named as "General Administration of State Railways and Ports" in 1927. Being administered as an annexed budget state enterprise until 1953, it became a State-Owned Enterprise in that year under the name "State Railways of the Turkish Republic (TCDD)". The railway policies were structured in accordance with national interests in the post-Republican period, providing a self-sufficient "national economy" was intended and it was aimed that the railways would stimulate the use of the sources of the country. The length of the railways in this period reached 9.204 km from 4.000 km, and in spite of all unfavorable conditions, building and administering railways were accomplished through national power (Anonymous 2010a).

The transportation policy of the Republican period expected the railway network to reach production centres and natural resources (Fig. 1). For example; the railway arriving to Ergani was named as the copper line, the one to Ereğli coalfield as the iron line and those to Adana and Çetinkaya were named as cotton and iron lines. With the centers of production and consumption, it was intended to establish the relations especially between ports and hinterlands. With the lines of Kalın-Samsun, Irmak and Zonguldak, the ports

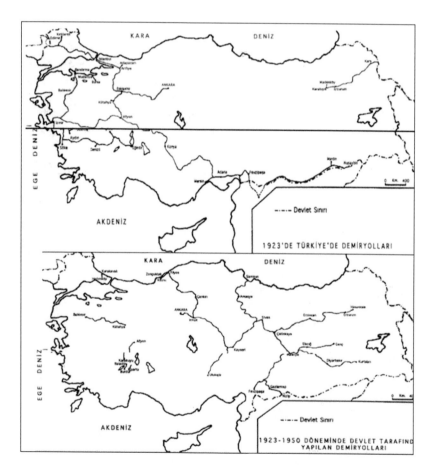

Fig.1. The Railway network built by foreign companies under the Ottoman rule and generalized during the Republican period (after: Yıldırım 2001: 209-211).

connected to railways raised to 8 from 6. With the Samsun and Zonguldak lines, the sea connections of Central and East Anatolia were reinforced (Anonymous 2010a).

To expand economic growth on a national level, the railways were intended to reach especially underdeveloped areas. While the political centre shifted from the West to Central Anatolia, the accessibility was extended to Central, East and Southeast Anatolia from the West. With respect to this policy; Kayseri in 1927, Sivas in 1930, Malatya in 1931, Niğde in 1933, Elazığ in 1934, Diyarbakır in 1935 and Erzurum in 1939 were linked to the railway network. With the intention of providing national security and integrity, the railways were aimed at cover the whole country.

To realize these targets, the railway transportation policy is regarded in two stages (Anonymous 2010a).

In the first stage, the railway lines held by foreign companies were nationalized by purchases despite great financial difficulties and a certain part was taken over through agreements. In the second stage, since a large part of the existing railway lines were concentrated at the West region, establishing the connection of the Middle and East areas with the centre and the coast was a target. In line with this purpose, it was ensured that mainlines were provided by the access of railway lines directly to centre of production. The mainlines made in this period were: Ankara-Kayseri-Sivas, Sivas-Erzurum (Kafkas line), Samsun-Kalın (Sivas), Irmak-Filyos (Zonguldak coal line), Adana-Fevzipaşa-Diyarbakır (Copper line), Sivas-Çetinkaya (Iron line). While 70% of the railways before the Republic remained at the east of the Ankara-Konya direction, the 78.6% of the routes were railed at the east during the Republican period and a proportional distribution as 46% and 54% is attained today for the west and east (Anonymous 2010a).

In addition, it was given importance to the production of branch lines, which linked mainlines and play an important role in spreading the railways country-wide. The construction of branch lines was extremely important in terms of national security. The branch lines were tried to be provided in 1935-45. The network type railways in the beginning of the Republic have contained two cycles in 1935 which consist of Manisa-Balıkesir-Kütahya-Afyon and Eskişehir-Ankara-Kayseri-Kardeş Gediği-Afyon. The cycles of İzmir-Denizli-Karakuyu-Afyon-Manisa and Kayseri-Kardeş Gediği-Adana-Narlı-Malatya-Çetinkaya were attained. The cycles were provided by branch lines. Reducing physical and economic distance was also intended in making these branch lines. For instance; with the Çetinkaya-Malatya branch line, the distance between Ankara and Diyarbakır was reduced from 1324 km to 1116 km and a change of 208 km was provided. Through these connections, the railways formed as a "tree" by the 19th century semi-colony economy transformed to a form of "network making cycles" which was entailed by the national economy. In the transportation policies implemented until 1950, highways were seen as a system that would feed and complete the railways. But in a period that highways needed to be developed in a way to complete and support the railways, constructing highways was started by almost neglecting railways along with the Marshall Plan. In this period in which the US was influential on the Turkish economy by means of the Marshall Plan, a process of industrialization particularly based on agricultural and consumer goods prevailed in the economic structure (Anonymous 2010a).

2.1.1.3. Agricultural policy

In order to develop the agriculture in the period of 1923-1950, many measures were taken under the guidance of the state. The primary objective in the agricultural development policy was to encourage all the small-large private agricultural production units.

By the enactment of the Civil Code after the Republic, the land ownership in the Ottomans called Miri System finished its evolution towards private ownership in the Ottoman society and was abolished. The subject of agriculture referred under the scope of economy policies in the Izmir Economy Congress originated the agricultural policy of the Republican period. The chronological order of the policies of agriculture and organization from the establishment of the Republic to 1945 are given below:

- The ashar tax was abolished with the "Law on the Tax to be Substituted with the Repeal of Ashar" dated February 17th, 1341 (1925) and numbered 552.
- At the Economy Congress on 17 February-4 March 1923, the "Turkish Farmers Association" was established under the guidance of agricultural engineers.
- "The Law on Fiduciary Agricultural Cooperatives" was enacted on April 21st, 1924 with the number 498. With this law, the Fiduciary Agricultural Cooperatives were expected to undertake particularly credits and other agricultural functions.
- "The Law on Agricultural Sale and Credit Cooperatives" was passed in 1935 with the encouragement of Atatürk and hence the state was assigned important duties and was empowered to resolve the problems of the rural areas.
- In order to conduct the agricultural support policy, the Ministry of Agriculture was established in 1937, the Soil Products Office in 1938, the Turkish Agricultural Equipment Institution (TZDK) in 1944 and the state has substantially enhanced its activity in agricultural input and output markets.
- "The Land Distribution Law" was enacted in 1945 (Çıkın and Karacan 1994).

The most crucial tax reform in the agricultural sector during the Republican period was the abolishment of ashar which was collected as a tax-in-kind and conversion of all taxes in this sector to monetary taxes. This important shift in the tax system led the agricultural sector to get out of a closed economic structure and thus agricultural products were oriented to the market in order to meet the need of cash (Topuz 2007: 367-380). With the Fiduciary Agricultural Cooperatives Regulations in 1924, the credit problem of the farmers was addressed. The Ziraat Bank (Agricultural Bank) was authorized to undertake the leading role in the agricultural sector and perform any bank activity in addition to agricultural credits. To import agricultural vehicles by means of the Ziraat Bank and deliver them to the producers without customs fees in order to provide mechanization in agriculture became a law in 1923. While the share of the agricultural sector was 44.4% in the GDP with the abolition of the ashar tax in 1925, this rate increased to 49.6% in 1926. In the ongoing depression of 1929 and the economic policies required to be followed, the Republican Turkey expected three separate functions to be fulfilled by the agriculture. These were to provide the national subsistence, to feed the national industry with necessary raw materials in accordance with its circumstances and future needs, and enhance exports to create foreign currency required for the industrial development (Sümer 1948: 4). The most prominent characteristic of this period is that all the measures were giving the desired outcomes. The Turkish economy which was a huge rural economy had started to gain a modern appearance although it gradually and was directed toward a bright future with its infrastructure and its industry in progress. The First Five-Year Industry Plan (1933-1937) promulgated in parallel with these goals was completely realized (Hatipoğlu and Aysan 1994: 18).

After establishment of the Republic, the attempts to change the land ownership distribution and provide fundamental reforms in the economic and social structure were undertaken in 1935s. The Settlement and Land Law prepared by the Ministry of Interior granted extensive powers to the major administrators. Atatürk's words in his speeches during the openings of the Grand National Assembly of Turkey (TBMM) in 1936 and 1937 declaring that the preparations are completed and the Land Law shall be submitted to the TBMM for approval and his thoughts were available (Aksoy 1971). But these couldn't be materialized due to the death of Atatürk and the interference of the Second World War. The School of Agriculture became the "Agricultural High Institute" with the law of 16th June 1933 numbered 2291. The year 1933 when the Agricultural High Institute was established is also the year of the university reform in Turkey. The "Dry Farming Experimental Station" was established in Eskişehir in 1931. In addition, some experiments were carried out to compare the costs of ploughings made by tractors and horses in dry farming as from 1935 at the 2.000 hectare Çifteler demonstration farm 45 km distant from Eskişehir. With the law of 1st January 1938 numbered 3308, the State Agricultural Enterprises Institution was formed to manage these farms established by Atatürk in various places of the country. Provisions about where and how tobacco should be sowed were included in the "Tobacco and Tobacco Monopoly Law" with the law numbered 3437 and enacted on 10 June 1938 (Tekeli and İlkin 1988: 43-53). The first interference in agricultural products in Turkey started with the "Wheat Protection Law" enacted in 1932 with law numbered 2056 and the Soil Products Office (TMO) was established as an economic state enterprise on 24.06.1938 with the law numbered 3491 as a result of the negotiations at the Turkish Grand National Assembly (Başol 1994: 121). The TMO has delivered grains to regions where there is no grain production or is not sufficient. After the TMO started its activities, no grain shortage or price increases or reductions as a result of grain abundance occurred in any region of Turkey.

It is seen that the biggest proportion in the GDP in 1931 with constant prices belongs to the agricultural sector with a rate of 49.1%. In this period of great depression of the entire world economy and with substantial decreases of real incomes in the capitalist countries, the agricultural sector has performed a pace of development in spite of all adverse circumstances (Boratav 1997). The Second World War (1939-1945) has started in the years following the death of Atatürk in 1938 and the war has had serious negative effects on our economic development.

The National Protection Law was passed in 1940 and later with the coordination decision numbered 477; the Ministry of Agriculture was given the authority to do agriculture on uncultivated public lands on behalf of the state. As the result on institutionalization of the mechanization of agriculture and the use of technical information, a new enterprise was established on 28th January 1943 with the law numbered 2/19373 and named "Decree on Formation of the Turkish Agricultural Equipment Institution". This institution has been one the main mechanisms for the agricultural mechanization movement that would accelerate (Tekeli and İlkin 1988: 43-53).

After the Second World War, the draft law on "Distributing Soil to Farmers and Establishing Farmers Soils" that was expected to be based on a land reform in the country was submitted to the parliament. According to the draft, the law was intended to give soil to farmers who have no or little land, to ensure cultivation of agricultural fields of the country permanently and prevent land ownership to grow extremely or go down below a certain rate. The TBMM enacted the draft with the "Law of Giving Soil to the Farmer" of 11.06.1945 and with law no. 4753 (Karluk 1997). In this period, stagnation and even a decline was witnessed in the economy of the country and the agricultural sector suffered.

2.1.1.4. Institutions and laws within the scope of planning and conservation

In the Republic era new institutional arrangements were established with the laws enacted between 1930 and 1935 for changing legislation remaining from the Ottoman Empire. These arrangements were "Municipal Law" numbered 1580, which was enacted in 1930 and obliged the municipalities to make plans, "General Hygiene Law" numbered 1593 and "Municipal Bank Establishment Law" numbered 2033 enacted in the same year. It was aimed to modernize the cities where Anatolian government enterprises were established and the other important settlements. With this aim, 1/500 scale implementation plans were including main artery roads, Cumhuriyet (Republic) Squares where the arter roads end, Government Offices and other governmental institution buildings in the historical centers of the cities (Dinçer and Akın 1994: 127-131). "The Law on Municipal Buildings and Roads" numbered 2290, which was accepted on June 10th, 1933 and published on June 21st, 1933, highlighted conservation of buildings with their surroundings (Akozan 1977: 24-52), provided a comprehensive planning approach with the population forecast concept it introduced (Dinçer and Akın 1994: 127-131), highlighted the requirement of a special planning in the areas including dense historical values, moreover it proposed a 10 meters gap (building approach limit) around the historical monuments. After diffusion of the consciousness on conservation of architectural monuments through development plans, the principles of respectful planning of historical and natural values gained importance. "The Law on Municipal Expropriation" dated 2722 and enacted in 1934 and "The Law on the Establishment of Municipal Development Commission" numbered 2763 and dated 1935 were important legal regulations (Tekeli 1998). The "General Ordinance of Regulating City

Development Plans" enacted in 1936 was a law effective in forming urban spaces through standardizing city plans and authorizing architects instead of survey engineers.

The first real urban conservation attempt was seen in Ankara Development Plan prepared by H. Jansen and approved on July 23th, 1932; the plan foreseen conservation and observation of the Citadel as the symbol of the national life and the Citadel and the vicinity was put under protection as a protocol site in 1937. "Municipal Development Commission" under The Ministry of Internal Affairs and "Urban Science Commission" under the Ministry of Public Works are the implementing and auditing institutions of the period (Dinçer and Akın 1994: 127-134).

With the arrangements made, "The Bank of Provinces" was established with the Law numbered 4759 in 1945. This Institutions, aiming to provide technical and financial support to the Municipalities in planning and infrastructure projects, had the capacities in that period but became incapable of responding the major transformations in the city in time (Tekeli 1998). It was aimed to increase the municipal incomes via "The Law on Municipal Income" numbered 5237 and enacted in 1948; however, municipal incomes failed to satisfy the significant transformation in the cities.

2.2. Republic cities

2.2.1. Lorcher-Jansen Plan of Ankara

The main and priority policy of the new formation process, aiming at an independent and modern society, a nation-state upon the establishment of the Republic, was the creation of the national bourgeoisie (Arıtan 2008). Ankara, which was declared as the capital on October 13th, 1923 within this policy framework and turned into "administrative" center of the New Republic, is created by the stated in terms of its spatial development.

Growing population in parallel to the developments in the new Capital necessitated planning of settlement areas and intense planning activities started with the idea that impeccable development of Ankara, as a symbol, was going to be identified with the success of the regime. The first step was establishment of the Municipality of Ankara with the Law on Ankara Municipality dated February 16th, 1924 and Numbered 417. Another step was the Expropriation Act enacted on March 24th, 1925 and numbered 583. Within the scope of this Law, the expropriation right for an area of 400 hectares (Sıhhiye) between south of the railway and Çankaya was given to the Municipality of Ankara with the purpose of establishing new settlement neighborhoods. Consequently, four types of housing patterns emerged in Ankara, which was divided into two with the expropriation law after 1925. These housing patterns were new apartments in the old urban pattern, villas in Yenişehir, public housing and old pattern (Demet 2010).

The first planning attempts for Ankara started by Heussler firm, for Old Ankara (the Citadel and its vicinity) in 1924 and for Yenişehir in 1925 with the plan made by Berliner architect Dr. Carl Ch. Lorcher, who was a member of Istanbul Development Commission. The old city plan was rejected as it was considered unimplementable, while the New City Plan, known also as Lorcher Plan, covering 150 hectares around the place known as Sıhhiye today was implemented. Lorcher Plan, named also as the first plan of Ankara, included the main decisions regarding Kızılay and its vicinity, which is a symbolic center of the city today (Sargın 2014; Demet 2010).

Lorcher Plan proposed a homogenous pattern including single and maximum two-floor buildings with gardens on a grid-iron road system. Despite implementation of this plan, the city development trend was towards Çankaya and Kecioren at the end of 1927. Lorcher Plan supports both th physical and organizational models of the city. Zoning based modern urban planning approach, the urban corridor which was proposed in Train Station-Ulus-Sıhhiye- Kızılay triangle to establish the urban integrity, urban stratification proposing integration with nature, new open public spaces designed to encourage public participation are major components of 1924-25 Plan. Especially the corridor starting in the Old-Town and

Fig.2. Ankara Public Plan of Prof. Hermann Jansen
(1932) (after: Jansen 1937; Tunçer 2009).

reaching to the New-Town passing through Sıhhiye and Zafer (Victory) Square integrates the public spaces and forms the face of the New-Town as it should be. This publicity starting from Millet (Ulus today) Square and ending in Cumhuriyet/Kurtuluş (Kızılay today) has undertaken very important tasks. For example, Ulus (Taşhan) Square is the final version of a new formation extending beyond the boundaries of the Old Town, is a commercial area for the public, an administrative center of the structures of centralizing Ottoman organization, and ideological hearth of the new formation in which the intellectual foundations of the nation-state was laid during the war. The square is a sub-urban part merging urban, military and administrative centers. On the other hand, Ulus Square undertook a much more important task during and after the war. It is a pioneer public space of the Republic and a starting point for modern Ankara, which was returning into a Capital (Sargın 2014; Demet 2010).

A development plan was needed for the Capital to be planned in a manner worthy of the prestige of the Republic, to achieve the objectives regarding modernity and to solve the problems of the city growing with a 6% population increase and a development plan competition was arranged within this framework (Tekeli 2009). German Prof. M. Brix, Herman Jansen and chief architect of the French Government Jean Jausseley participated in the Ankara Master Plan Competition hold in 1927 and the Prof. Herman Jansen was declared as the winner in 1928. Jansen Plan proposed an average density of 120-240 person/hectare in 1500 ha area for a population of 300.000 (Fig.2). Main objectives of the Jansen Plan, which brought an applicable realistic approach while protecting the Old Ankara were protection of the Citadel and its surroundings, expansion of the road connecting the Old Town to Çankaya (Atatürk Boulevard) as the main artery of the city in the north-south direction, establishing Ministerial estate including the Parliament and Ministry structures between the Old Town and Çankaya in the south, reserving the low elevation areas for outdoor sports and recreation usages such as Gençlik Park, 19 Mayıs Sports Complex and Hippodrome, utilization of high elevation areas such as the Citadel, Kocatepe, Hacettepe, Rasattepe, Maltepe and improving their visual aspects as viewpoints, establishing a green space system, establishing two main arteries crossing the city in the North-South (Atatürk Boulevard) and the East-West (Talat Paşa Boulevard) directions (Demet 2010).

Tankut (1993) summarizes the main principles of the Jansen Plan as follows:
-    Urban aesthetics is the primary concern of the plan. Ankara Citadel is a "city crown" which is the source of this aesthetics. According to Jansen, dominant factor in the urban economy is the savings to be achieved in the road construction. This could be achieved via constructing short, straight, narrow roads fitting the topography.
-    Urban health is provided via green spaces, sports fields, playgrounds, parks and open spaces.
-    Health aspects to be considered are low density of buildings with low number of floors and positioning the houses in a direction guided by the sun. Sewage and rainwater infrastructures should be resolved properly for a healthy environment.
-    Reasons of various land uses and their functions are explained under the title of grouping of urban spaces. For example, residential areas divided into 18 regions and a separate development plan is

proposed for each. In general, Jansen foresaw maximum 3 floors for Ankara and designs detached and separate houses. Jansen's buildings have front and backyard gardens weather they are blocks or single houses. The most prominent examples of this system are large villas in spacious gardens and single or rowed worker houses on small plots.

- Selection of industrial areas is based on two criteria. Accessibility and predominant wind direction are the reasons of allocation of the vicinity of the station in the west for this purpose.

- The least land use information is given about the commercial areas. First of all, there is no "commercial center" concept in Jansen's competition annotations. Jansen considers the citadel as the city center and being content with a physical-visual center, he disregards the functional city center. However, in 1928 competition project, a huge are between İstasyon Street and the station is allocated for commercial purposes. It is described as the shops area in the German legend. This arrangement is changed in 1932 plan; Genclik Park replaces the shops area. In the area determined for the competition, a commercial zone was not determined for the commercial needs of Yenisehir. Old bazaar of the old town was obliged to serve the New City but this was not mentioned in the development plan note. Sub-commercial zones were not determined spatially for the New Town. Istasyon Street and commercial area proposed in the concept project of Jansen is suitable for industrialized western urban model.

- Jansen proposed very few principles under the heading of transport. The north-south and the east-west connections of Ankara were already given to the competitors as historical data. Additionally, secondary roads designed by Lörcher were also available. Jansen was aiming to control the traffic and economize via the limitations on the transportation network. The pedestrian paths passing through the green belts were designed both to provide the interior connection of Ankara and to curtain the nuisance of the traffic. This was introduced as an element of urban health (Tankut 1993).

In to the Jansen Plan, the city was intended to developed as a circular form surrounding the Citadel, including neighborhoods separated with green belts, with a transport connection based on a backbone connection road (Ataturk Boulevard) between the old and the new city and secondary roads supporting the circular shape (Günay 2006: 72). The Plan shows a modern design connecting different functional zones the city (Fig. 3).

Bahcelievler Building Society, formed according to Jansen Plan in 1934, is an important example in Turkish Planning history as the first building society of the country. Turkish Cooperative Association was established on May 20th, 1931. The association was moved to Ankara in 1933. In June of the same year, the cooperative was given the opportunity to act in the non-agricultural lands. Bahcelievler Building Society was formed within this framework and was developed by the experts of the period Nusret Uzgören, Affan Ataçeri, Fethi Aktan, Cenap And and Sabit Sağıroğlu. These buildings, which were planned as a reflection of "the garden city" approach developed in the UK, were the most important initiatives designed for different life demands (Fig.4). The society is composed of 169 detached and single mass housing units (Karaaslan and Eril 2001).

During the period between 1928 Jansen Competition Project and the approval of the "Final Development Plan" on July 23th, 1932, the core of the Plan was oriented from the Citadel to Cankaya, which created difference such as Kızılay Square, as the traditional urban pattern was left unregulated. It could be said that certain elements of the Jansen Plan was implemented in the initial years. However, in the following year, the Plan lost its true nature due to the obstacles faced in the implementation of the development plans, land speculation and rapid growth of the city (Demet 2010).

After the 2nd World War, like all over the world, especially big cities went under the pressure of migrating population from the rural due to the increasing urbanization in Turkey. Development of Ankara city could not be controlled due to rapid population increase and the lack of the required enforcements in the Jansen plan decisions, consequently the population target of 300.000 inhabitants in 1978 was reached at the beginning of 1950s. "Squatter Housing" phenomenon emerged, marking the city, in the second half of the 1940s (Karaaslan and Eril 2001).

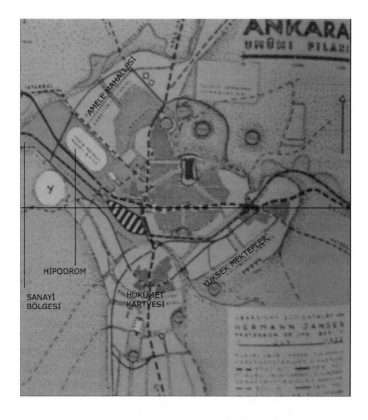

Fig.3. Functional zones in the city in the Jansen Plan (after: Günay 2006: 72).

Fig.4. Bahcelievler Building Society (after: Kansu 2009)

2.2.2. Guvenpark–Guven (Trust) Monument

Guvenpark, which reflects the ideology of the Republic Period, is on the Sıhhıye-Ulus side of Vekaletler Neighborhood, designed on a triangle shaped land by Clemens Holzmeister, an Austrian architect who is also designed many buildings in Bakanlıklar (the Ministries) area (Ertuna 2005: 6-15). The axis starting from Guven Monument is surrounded by the Ministerial buildings placed symmetrically when exiting the park and is designed as a continuous pedestrian arterial road which ends at the Parliament Building (Anonymous 2004: 352; Ayoğlu 2010).

The theme of the Monument in this area, which represents the Republic, is determined as "the police and gendarmerie" and it is dedicated to the police organization with the aim of monumentalization of the security forces (Şenyapılı 2004: 213). The article titled "How wills the Police Monument Be?" published in Hakimiyet-i Milliye (National Sovereignty) newspaper dated December 2nd, 1929 explained that "the public is represented with the family as the unit of the society in the monument. A peaceful and happy family in the middle and gendarmerie around them countering the attacks and struggling with the criminal to maintain their happiness is represented via allegoric groups. Although the name of the Police Monument refers to security forces, the main idea of the monument is the family as the core of the society aimed by the Republic. The things changed when the monument was finished were not only words replaced due to the Language Revolution, but also the main idea of the monument. There was still a referral to the security forces in Guven (Trust) Monument, but the monument reflected the "protection" reflex with the abstract figures with no referral to national and historical context (Aydin et al. 2005: 719)

The Monument is designed two-sided on the north-south direction via the alternative use of vertical and horizontal blocks and the base. The base of the Monument is 37 meters long, the central block is with a height of 8 meters, side wings with a height of 2 meters and the bronze figures are 6 meters. On one side of the composition, Old and Young Turks figures are placed separate from the main block, representing the past and the future of Turkey and the words of Ataturk "Turks be proud, work and trust" are located under these figures. On the lower reliefs, Turkish villagers carrying guns to the front, the health care team working in the hinterland for the victory, efforts of security officials for the safety of the public, artists, philosophers, various professional groups, blacksmiths, miners, artisans, and potters are represented (Anonymous 2004: 352; Ayoğlu 2010).

The protocol axis proposed by Holzmeister in his project from the Monument to the Parliament, which is fragmented today, aimed at highlighting intermingling of the rulers and the ruled. This artery road has occasionally been closed to the pedestrians due to the protests on the protocol road in the recent past. However, it is open to the traffic and Eskisehir road passes between the Ministries and the Parliament (Anonymous 2004: 352; Ayoğlu 2010).

In the Jansen Plan, the park covers an area of 25.000 m² (Anonymous 2004: 352; Ayoğlu 2010). Guvenpark became a majestic focal point of New Ankara as a public space after the construction of the Monument. The Monument became one of the main stops of the school trips and an entertainment venue where the youth meets with their guitars and accordions on summer nights. Furthermore, the vendors were prohibited to pass beyond Suhhiye Railroad Bridge to Kızılay side before eight in the morning to maintain this decent state of the area and the bridge became not only an administrative but also a social barrier between the new and the old town. In parallel to the changing face of Kızılay after its declaration as a business district, the building density and height around Guvenpark started to increase as a result of the decisions in 1957 Yucel-Uybadin Development Plan (Ertuna 2005: 6-15).

The Monument lost its magnificent impact during its initial years due to the deterioration in its proportional relation with the surrounding environment. Symbolic importance and visual perception features of Guvenpark and Guven Monument are destroyed with billboards, decorative elements and the so-called spatial arrangements (Ayoğlu 2010). The historical transformation in proportional relation of the Monument with its environment is presented in Fig.5.

Fig.5. Guven (Trust) Monument from Past to Present
(after: Anonymous 2010b)

2.3. The Prost Plan of Istanbul

After urban development activities started in Ankara in 1933, Byzantine churches which were used as mosques after conquest of İstanbul were decided to be turned into museums. After this decision, it was aimed to prepare a master development plan for İstanbul which aims to protect the monuments reflecting Byzantine and Ottoman history and architectural identity. Within this framework, famous French urban planner Henri Prost was invited to Istanbul by the Turkish government. At the time, Istanbul consisted of three main old settlements: Historical Peninsula on both sides of Golden Horn and Galata, Uskudar and Kadıkoy on Asian side (Aydemir 2008).

In order to prevent the chaos created by rapid development of the city and increasing number of vehicles, solutions to arrange the transportation network, building new artery road, conserving worldwide known buildings and archaeological artifacts required critical, sensitive and specialized planning activities.

Initial works of Prost aimed at conservation and usage of the historical skyline and historical monuments of Istanbul in their own environment. In line with this purpose, modernization without damaging natural and historical integrity of Istanbul, providing transportation infrastructure, and revealing architectural and archaeological values formed the main frameworks of Prost Plan. Within this framework, master plan is evaluated as Historical Peninsula and Beyoglu (Fig.6). Integration of the north and south of Golden Horn was aimed. Furthermore, a road connecting the Centre to settlement area starting from Galata Bridge, passing through ferry port Kabatas and reaching to Sarıyer, and a coast road passing through the hills of phosphorus and connecting the settlements (Büyükdere-Taksim) are proposed (Aydemir 2008).

The main artery roads sourcing from Taksim Square aimed at connecting Beyoglu to Historical Peninsula. First artery includes a tunnel up to Galata Tower, passes the bridge to Beyazıt Square and reaches to Topkapı Palace with a wide street from this area. The second road starting from Taksim passed through the unhealthy neighborhoods of Pera (Beyoglu) and rehabilitated this area. Moreover, the road was constructed with the aim of connecting Golden Horn to Marmara, Beygolu to settlement areas in Historical Peninsula. In the development plan of Historical Peninsula, two roads were proposed passing the hills in the middle of the Peninsula and in line with the axis created during the period of Constantine the Emperor. One of the roads started from Topkapı Palace and Haghia Sophia and reaches to Edirnekapı passing through Beyazıt, while the other reaches to Topkapı Palace through Universite (University) Square. Today, both the streets exist (Vatan-Millet Street). Additionally, a wide coastal road connecting the areas between the end Ataturk Boulevard and Sarayburnu and Bakırkoy was proposed in the same plan. Moreover, regional arrangements, which are very important in terms of art history and tourism, including the commercial zones, inns and historical monuments between Eminonu and Beyazıt are partially implemented (Eminonu-New Mosque- Covered Bazaar- Spice Bazaar) (Aydemir 2008). A 20 hectares large park among Macka, Harbiye, Taksim and Dolmabahce was proposed in the plan prepared for Beyoglu. The park project included entertainment centers, an open-air theatre, a sports hall and exhibition halls, a seaside square next to Dolmabahce Palace where important guests are welcomed and huge green areas for sports competitions

The project was implemented despite the harsh conditions of the period. H. Prost started to work on a subway project in 1943 considering the rapid population increase. The project aimed at connecting Beyoglu and Historical Istanbul (the subway is under construction today) (Aydemir 2008).

H. Prost conserved the traces and monuments of four great Civilizations (Byzantin-Roman-Byzantine-Ottoman) which had great impact on Europe, Roman, Byzantium and Ottoman Places, Hagia Sophia, Hippodrome, Little Hagia Sophia, Sarayburnu Park and Topkapı Palace in the regions bounded by the Sea of Marmara.

Prost Plan resulted in some problems, despite its aim of protection and usage principle and its success in implementing the decisions. Allocation of Goldern Horn and Marmara costs to commercial and industrial activities resulted in environmental pollution in Goldern Horn and Yedikule, while preservation of Sirkeci

Fig.6. Henry Prost Plan, 1937 (Gürer and Tuncer 2006: 304-306).

Railway Station as a suburban station, international station and port arrangements in Yenikapı and construction of three main roads in Historical Peninsula (Vatan, Millet Streets, Sirkeci-Florya coastal road) led to loss of historical identity at a large extent (İBB 2003: 36).

3. CONCLUSIONS

Modernization policies of the Republic includes large scale development planning, transportation and landscape works at rural scale, while they include modernist centralized urban planning activities at the urban scale. Kemalism, as a part of modernity project, undertook the duty to build the nation-state, aimed at turning the country space into a nation-state space and making the city the place of modernity.

Accordingly, Ankara city is planned in a way to represent the republic regime with the Jansen Plan, while Prost Plan of Istanbul aimed at protecting the historical and natural features of the city. Works done within this context are implemented successfully despite the conditions of the period and became revolutionary.

BIBLIOGRAPHY

Akın, T., Kejanlı, T. and Yılmaz, A. (2007). Türkiye'de koruma yasalarının tarihsel gelişimi üzerine bir inceleme. *Elektronik Sosyal Bilimler Dergisi,* 6(19): pp. 250-267.

Akozan, F. (1977). *Türkiye'de Tarihi Anıtları Koruma Teşkilâtı ve Kanunlar,* D.G.S.A. Yayını, 47, İstanbul, pp. 24-52.

Aksoy, S. (1971). *100 Soruda Türkiye'de Toprak Meselesi,* Gerçek Yayınevi, İstanbul.

Anonymous, 2004. *Ankara Başkentin Tarihi, Arkeolojisi ve Mimarisi.* Ankara Enstitüsü Vakfı Yayınları, Ankara: pp. 352.

Anonymous, 2010a. Cumhuriyet dönemi demiyolu ve karayolları. http://www.bakterim.net/

Anonymous, 2010b. Ankara-eski fotoğraflar başlıklı forum girdisi. Wow Turkey Web Sitesi. [online: http://wowturkey.com/forum/viewtopic.php?t=557]

Arıtan, Ö. (2008). Modernleşme ve cumhuriyetin kamusal mekan modelleri. *Mimarlık Dergisi,* Temmuz-Ağustos.

Aydemir, I. (2008). İki Fransız mimarı Henri Prost ve August Perret'nin İstanbul ile ilgili çalışmaları. *Yıldız Teknik Üniversitesi Mimarlık Fakültesi E Dergi Megaron:* 3,1 İstanbul.

Aydın, S., Emiroğlu, K., Türkoğlu, Ö. and Özsoy, E.D. (2005). *Küçük Asya'nın Bin Yüzü:* Ankara. Dost Kitabevi Yayınları, Ankara, p. 719.

Ayoğlu, B.O. (2010). *"Zafer Anıtı-Güvenpark- TBMM" Kent Aksinin Var olan Durumunun İrdelenmesi ve Cumhuriyet Aksi Olarak Yeniden Tasarımı,* Msc. Ankara University.

Başol, K. (1994). *Türkiye Ekonomisi,* Anadolu Matbaası, İzmir, p. 121.

Bilgin, İ. (1998). *Modernleşmenin ve Toplumsal Hareketliliğin Yörüngesinde Cumhuriyetin İmarı, 75 Yılda Değişen Kent ve Mimarlık,* Ed. Yıldız Sey, T. İş Bank. Kült. Yay. ve Tarih Vakfı, İstanbul, pp. 255-272.

Bilsel, C. (2009). İzmir'de Cumhuriyet dönemi planlaması (1923-1965): 20. Yüzyıl Kentsel Mirası. *Ege Mimarlık,* Ekim, pp. 12-17.

Birol, G. (2004). Bir Batı Anadolu kasabasının modern bir kente dönüşümünün hikayesi, pp.1940-1960 Yılları Arasında Balıkesir'de İmar Etkinliklerine Genel Bir Bakış. *Ege Mimarlık* İzmir sayı, p. 51.

Boratav, K. (1997). *Türkiye İktisat Tarihi 1908–1985,* IV. Cilt, Cem Yayınevi İstanbul.

Çelebican, G. (1982). "Atatürk Döneminde Para-Kredi Siyaseti ve Kurumlaşma Hareketi", *Atatürk Dönemi Ekonomi Politikası ve Türkiye'nin Ekonomik Gelişmesi Semineri,* A.Ü. Siyasal Bilgiler Fakültesi Yayınları, Ankara, pp. 23-34.

Çıkın, A. and Karacan, A.R. (1994). *Genel Kooperatifçilik.* EÜZF Yayın No: 511, Bornova, İzmir.

Demet, E. (2010). *Kentsel Politikalar Ders Notları.* Gazi Üniversitesi Mimarlık Fakültesi Şehir Bölge Planlama Bölümü, Ankara.

Dinçer, İ. and Akın, O. (1994). "Kültür ve Tabiat Varlıklarını Koruma Kapsamında Koruma Planı ve İdari Yapısı", *2. Kentsel Koruma Yenileme ve Uygulama Kollokyumu,* İstanbul, pp. 127-131.

DPT (2010). Devlet Planlama Teşkilatı Resmi İnternet Sitesi [online: http://www.dpt.gov.tr]

Ertuna, C. (2005). *Kızılay'ın Modernleşme Sahnesinden Taşralaşmanın Sahnesine Dönüşüm Sürecinde Güvenpark ve Güvenlik Anıtı.* Planlama TMMOB. Şehir Plancıları Odası Yayını, 4, pp. 6-15.

Ezer, F. (2005). *1923-1938 Döneminde Türkiye'de Uygulanan İmâlat Ve Sanayi Politikaları.* Fırat Üniversitesi Fen-Edebiyat Fakültesi Tarih Bölümü, Doğu Anadolu Bölgesi Araştırmaları, Elazığ. Günay, B. (2006). *Ankara Çekirdek Alanının Oluşumu ve 1990 Nazım Planı Hakkında Bir Değerlendirme,* Cumhuriyet'in Ankara'sı (der.) T. Şenyapılı, ODTÜ Yayıncılık, Ankara, pp. 72.

Gürer, T.K. and Tuncer, E. (2006). Sağlık, Kent Planlama İlişkisi Bağlamında İstanbul Tarihi. *Yarımda Bölgesinin 19.yy. Kent Planlarının İncelenmesi Kent ve Sağlık Sempozyumu*, 07-09 Haziran 2006 Bursa, pp. 304-306.

Hatipoğlu, Z. and Aysan, M. (1994). *Türkiye Ekonomisinde 1994 Bunalımı*, Beta Basım Yayım Dağıtım A.Ş., İstanbul, pp. 18

İBB, (2003). *İstanbul Büyük Şehir Belediyesi Tarihi Yarımada Eminönü-Fatih 1/5000 Ölçekli Koruma Amaçlı Nazım İmar Planı Raporu*, I.Cilt, Planlama ve İmar Müdürlüğü, İstanbul, pp. 36.

İnan, A. (1972). *Devletçilik İlkesi ve Türkiye Cumhuriyetinin Birinci Sanayi Planı 1933*, Ankara: Türk Tarih Kurumu Basımevi.

Jansen, H. (1937), *"Ankara Şehri İmar Planı"*, Alaattin Kral Basımevi.

Kansu, U. (2009). Jansen'in Ankara'sı için Örnek Bir "Bahçe Şehir" ya da Siedlung: "Bahçeli Evler Yapı Kooperatifi 1934–1939" [online: www.mimdap.org/images/dosya/Yeni%20Klas%F6r/4.jp]

Karaaslan, Ş. and Eril, D. (2001) Ankara'da Farklı Gelir Gruplarının Barınma Beklentilerinin Konut Ve Çevresine Olan Etkileri BAP Projesi.

Karluk, R. (1997). *Türkiye Ekonomisi*, Beta Basım Yayım Dağıtım A.Ş., İstanbul.

Keyder, Ç. (1978). "1923-1929 Döneminde Para ve Kredi", Türkiye iktisadı üzerine araştırmalar, *Ortadoğu Teknik Üniversitesi Gelişme Dergisi:* Özel Sayısı, Ankara, pp. 210-250.

Olgun, Ç. (2003). Anadolu'da bir "Yarı-Çevre Modernite Deneyimi": Kemalizm şehirciliği. *Planlama Dergisi*, 3, pp. 14-3.

Sargın, A.G. (2014). Öncül kamusal mekânları tasarlamak: Başkent Ankara üzerine kısa notlar, 1923-1946. *Mülkiye Dergisi*, pp. 241.

Şenyapılı, Ö. (2004). *Ne demek Ankara; Balgat, niye Balgat!?..* ODTÜ Yayıncılık, Ankara, pp. 213.

Sümer, M. (1948). "Yurdumuzun zirai kalkınması", *Tarım Bakanlığı Dergisi*, 10.

Şengül, T. (2009). *Kentsel Çelişki ve Siyaset. Kapitalist Kentleşme Süreçlerinin Eleştirisi*, İmge Yayınevi, İstanbul.

Tankut, G. (1990). *Bir Başkentin İmarı, Ankara:* ODTÜ Mimarlık Fakültesi Yayını.

Tankut, G. (1993). *Bir Başkentin İmarı (1929-1939)*, Anahtar Yayınları, 26, 46, 79, İstanbul.

Tanyeli, U. (1998). *Türkiye'de Mimari Modernleşmenin Büyük Dönemeci (1900-1930)*, Arredamento Mimarlık, pp. 64-67.

Tekeli, İ. and İlkin, S. (1982). *Uygulamaya Geçerken Devletçiliğin Oluşumu*, Ankara.

Tekeli, İ. (1984). *"Ankara'nın Başkentlik Kararının Ülkesel Mekan Organizasyonu ve Toplumsal Yapıya Etkileri Bakımından Genel Bir Değerlendirilmesi"*, Tarih İçinde Ankara, Eylül 1981 Seminer Bildirileri, ODTÜ Mim. Fak. Basım İşliği, Ankara.

Tekeli, İ. and İlkin, S. (1988). Türkiye'de Tarımsal Yapılar 1923–2000. Yurt Yayınları. pp. 43–53.

Tekeli, İ. (1998). *Türkiye'de Cumhuriyet Döneminde Kentsel Gelişme ve Kent Planlaması, 75 Yılda Değişen Kent ve Mimarlık Bilanço'98*, Tarih Vakfı Yayınları, İstanbul.

Tekeli, İ. (2008). *Türkiye'de Bölgesel Eşitsizlik ve Bölge Planlama Yazıları.* Tarih Vakfı Yurt Yayınları, İstanbul.

Tekeli, İ. (2009). *Modernizm, Modernite ve Türkiye'nin Kent Planlama Tarihi.* Tarih Vakfı Yurt Yayınları, İstanbul.

Tezel, Y.S. (1994). *Cumhuriyet Döneminin İktisadi Tarihi*, İstanbul.

Topuz, M. (2007). *Cumhuriyet Dönemi Ekonomisinde Tarımsal Yapının İncelenmesi*, Süleyman Demirel Üniversitesi, İktisadi ve İdari Bilimler Fakültesi C.12 S.3 Isparta, pp. 367-380.

Tunçer., M. (2009). Cumhuriyet'in "Mimari Mirası"nın Planlama Aracılığı İle Korunması: Ankara Örneği,*TMMOB Mimarlar Odası Cumhuriyet'in Mimari Mirası Sempozyumu*, 26-27.02.2009. [online: www.planlama.org/.../Makaleler/mtuncer

Yıldırım, İ. (2001). *Cumhuriyet Döneminde Demiryolları (1923-1950)*, AKDTYK, Atatürk Araştırma Merkezi, 17, 39, Ankara, pp. 209-211.